UNBREAKING MY LIFE

One man's journey through the prison of paralysis

ALEXANDER THOMAS SMITH

Paperback ISBN 13: 978-1-8380925-0-4
.epub eBook ISBN 13: 978-1-8380925-1-1
.mobi eBook ISBN 13: 978-1-8380925-2-8

Published by ATS Books

UNBREAKING MY LIFE:

One Man's Journey Through the Prison of Paralysis!

A Handbook on my Life Before and After Injury

Alexander Thomas Smith

CONTENTS

INTRODUCTION

This is the story of Alexander Thomas Smith, a typical man enjoying life until fatal injury takes away this ability in the form of paralysis from the chest down. The book holds his voice and the record of his recovery to date, although now he stands still in his recuperation.

This is a handbook on the thoughts, feelings and desires of a normal man trapped inside a body that's inactive – but his brain certainly is! It is scattered with random thoughts throughout that are honest, heartbreaking, thought provoking, heart-warming and occasionally overwhelming for the reader. The handbook also contains a diary section, which didn't start out life as such – it began as his sister's notebook to remember questions to ask the doctors, but became a diary from her to Alex so he could see how far he had come.

A handy safety reference section is included at the end all about autonomic dysreflexia (AD).

My name is Alexander Thomas Smith. I worked as a marine engineer and my real life story begins while I was out enjoying life in the Caribbean. On December 14th 2006 at 14:18 hrs, however, my life changed in an instant!

INJURY

During my leisure time away from MS Westerdam, the cruise ship I was working on as a Fourth Engineer, along with other crew members that day, I decided to go swimming while my friend was setting up the sunbeds. I jumped into the sea (Baywatch style), and as I went through the water I managed to hit a sandbank. Instantly, and all happening within 30 seconds, the weight of my body broke my own neck. I knew then that something was seriously wrong – as I tried to swim to the surface I felt as if I was actually swimming but my arms were just floating beside me. I could feel the heat of the sun on my back so I knew I was on the surface, but all I could do was shake my head! This drew the attention to my friends that I was in danger.

I remember the sand was snow white and the water crystal clear – so beautiful but so deadly...

While that may sound critical enough, the crux of this is that the vertebrae at C5 fractured and C6 broke into three parts, one of which damaged my spinal cord, leaving me paralysed from the nipples down.

This accident happened on the island of Sint Maarten. I was initially sent to the nearest hospital where the doctor from the cruise ship accompanied me. Once established that I had severe injuries I was flown to the Jackson Memorial Hospital in Miami. After many investigations it turned out that, along with a broken neck I had unfortunately ingested salt water into my lungs, which led to secondary drowning. Shortly afterwards I was medically induced into a coma, where I stayed for six weeks. During this time I 'flatlined' six times (an electrical time sequence measurement that shows no activity and therefore, when represented, shows a flat line instead of a moving one). As part of the surgery the temperature of my spine was reduced right down to 33° Celsius to prevent swelling and further paralysis; this in turn led to pneumonia/ hyperthermia.

Once out of my coma I was shortly moved to rehab. In total I spent 3½ months in Miami. (Please refer to my sister's diary for her account of events at this time also).

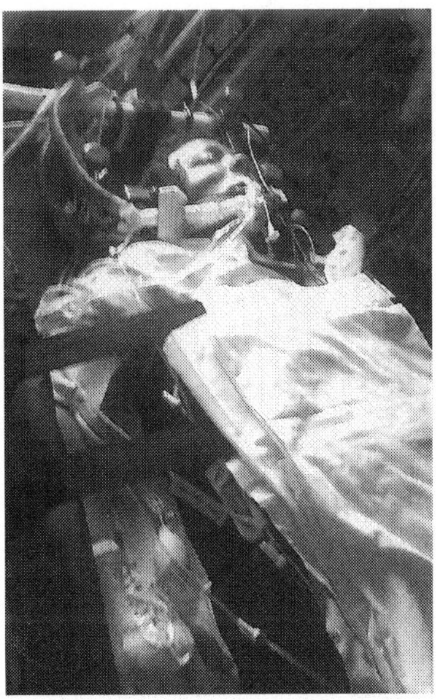

Receiving full life support, taken around December 21st

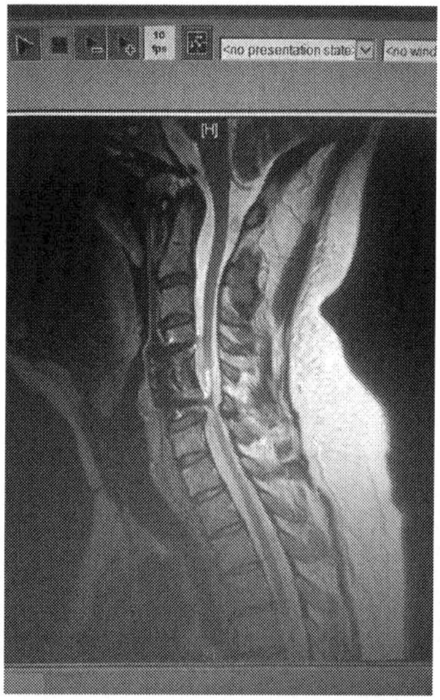

Shocking spinal MRI image which clearly shows my broken C5/C6

TREATMENT

I was flown back to the UK in March 2007, to the Royal Buckinghamshire Hospital in Aylesbury for a further 3½ months. I was lucky enough to get five hours' physio a day along with hydrotherapy 2–3 times a week – but like everything, it costs money... Once I was medically fit I moved home on the 20th of June 2007 with an RTI 300 FES bike. This bike warmed my muscles up for half an hour before the electricity kicked in and fired pulses into my legs, working them for me. This has helped maintain the muscle mass within my legs. I also had the upper torso part that works the biceps, triceps and shoulder muscles. Whilst the lower part works on the 'non-moving parts', the upper part would make me stronger and more independent. I also now own a standing chair, which allows me to work on blood pressure problems and balance while also helping to reactivate dormant muscles.

Twice a week I had physio at my home, up until November 2015. Unfortunately recovery stops when the money does. As with all my equipment it's the ongoing expense of which I need all the help I can, in the hope of walking again, although more about independence with walking later on (after nine years – 13 years to date!) I've been really lucky having been helped by those around me – family, friends and strangers alike. The whole of Galway, Ireland have been fundraising for me, as well as Holland America Line – a British–American-owned cruise line. There is also Regain – a sports injury charity helping tetraplegics lead independent and fulfilling lives. They have helped me no end with some very expensive equipment. Last but not least I will mention the agency, Viking Recruitment, the cruise ship specialists offering career opportunities globally. They were my employers and paramount in supporting me during and after my accident and also a key fundraiser, especially at the start of my treatment.

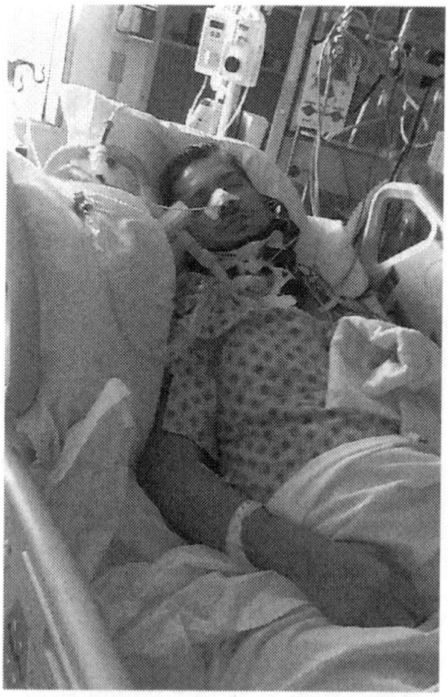

Still asleep, but this was taken after I'd awoken from the coma on January 8/9th 2007, before moving to rehab in Miami

THOUGHTS, FEELINGS AND MENTAL HEALTH

As you find yourself living every day with your injury, people forget the need and the power of just being outside and what it does for your soul.

This is not just a handbook on my life but an insight into the roads, the routes of my mind and the circle of life… My life of 13 years during which my mind was trapped, going round and round with uneasy thoughts and asking myself, Will it be this way until I'm in the ground? It's only me and myself that can change that… but not until time itself allows it. Maybe that time will stop ticking soon. Maybe not, only time will tell… reading this you may even start to see me holding on tight in this hurricane of pain!

As the wind takes me, my life will be what makes me!

Thoughts, fears and frustrations trapped in a body broken over ten years, a small insight to how my mind deals with paralysis.

The devil inside…

Your life is your own and yours alone in the choices you make; the risks we all take lead to the consequences we face. We can be the devil within ourselves. We create, live, love and loathe the one life we make for ourselves. Sometimes, by our own making, our lives become our very own hell! When your predicament has been caused by your own fault in life, your own making, your frustration can become paramount. Trapped in a cycle only we individually can change, some things set but some things like fluid will flow – those are ours to mould… to make… Life is suffering, death is eternal peace… Even so, we continue each day, only the strong go on. We only live for a blink of an eye in respect to the true time line that is life – it's all ultimately up to you unless tragic and cruel circumstances out of your control can make your life hell. It's when your own choices have made your life this way that they can beat you up inside. Only you can make the change and take that leap of faith. Faith only in one's self can make the devil inside turn and smile. Only you can create joy and bring love through the pain that is life and what we build for ourselves, for we create life, we live life. All we truly have inside ourselves is what we make – for you are the devil inside yourself!

I'm trapped in my broken body by my very own mistake. Although broken in this, the prison of paralysis, my mind is free to wander, free to make things better… but true to life my mind is free to torture me with the words, What if..? Why me..? if only for a brief moment in time. Your choices that you choose – you live the consequences. What you do defines the road ahead, for this is yours alone to take.

Make a difference… for you are the one living the life you have.

Frustration is my life – staying positive in a life of frustration – you tell me how? In 13 years I've achieved so much; I still breathe, I'm still here! I live by what has happened through these years, although things don't look good just now or last year… Earlier this year they didn't either… But at 14:18 hrs on December 14th 2006 and the following few weeks my life revolved around the fight to survive. My fight for my life didn't look good either, but I survived that – I'm still here! I don't know why but I am here, and for that reason alone I continue, thanks to those around me this year, I regained my freedom. Tonight, tomorrow or perhaps the day after I may find out why I am living through paralysis. But for now, my life is paralysis. I survived, so I continue!

It's your feelings inside that count and the outside world you can still see with your own eyes. Life is who you are, not just what you do each day. You let your thoughts out or keep them within… whatever you decide, it's your life!

Comparing my new life to my old life – my life. I lived an extreme life prior to injury, travelling whenever I felt the need with no real ties to up and leave; now I find myself living a strict routine with paralysis. Independence and freedom are a fleeting memory... but I'm always, always holding onto hope however distant. Nobody knows what will be – success in life cannot really be measured in monetary value or status in this world, but more with how you live inside yourself. Be happy with who you are, for wherever in this world you go 'you' will always be there.

I was just centimetres, millimetres away from paralysis. Paralysis is a bitch. Paralysis – you fuck!

HOPE

Everybody needs it and without it... why wake up the next day? I have hope... hope for what could be... what might be. Sometimes I feel I haven't moved on from what happened to me, I don't think you ever could. The day 'I stopped moving' – that moment in time will stay with me forever, no matter what, but instead of, What if..? or What could have been, it's now What might be and What could be. It's still ME!

Time waits for no man.

As time slips away each day, somehow life continues... I continue onto a future unknown!

My body stuck, my mind free... free in a body broken, holding onto the hope of something. Hold onto your heartstrings, people, they are the pathway to your soul, the energy inside yourself... it's where you store that hope.

Hope is all we have, lose it and we lose ourselves.

Beauty is fleeting... Like a rose on a fence sitting in a wind tunnel, that is life. It comes from the earth to blossom through a branch of thorns; the beauty within is undeniable, even with all the effort put into getting it there, the wind blows. The petals fall and the flower loses itself from the outside in.

A puppy lives and loves and holds no grudge. He lives

a short life and leaves, but in that life leaves a life full of love. Any life lost leaves a hole but all the suffering in life is worth that time spent loving. That moment of beauty held in your heart forever, life is worth living because it's only through all the pain that you finally see the true beauty that life hides. Suffer a lifetime for a moment of love, that moment is then yours forever.

Where there's life there's hope, and if the slightest glimmer of hope is apparent there's still life to live, be that my life or yours – hope beyond any possibility as any hope. All hope is life and every life is built around hope. Without it we are nothing, but with it we can be anything, do anything.

Every day I continue with the pain that is life… Why and to what end – who knows? Up and down, each day the same with no end to a never ending cycle of pain. Even through all this I still each day wake up and continue thinking that 'the only true freedom is in death', but each and every one of us has survival ingrained into them! Get onto that dark road and it's extremely difficult to find your way back... but in the darkness the slightest spark will light your way. Although others may be able to guide you, you enter and exit this world alone, so too is your life down to you! However restricted, however small the changes, however you make each step is down to you.

Each and every one of us is built to survive through pain with hope. While there still exists joy, love and understanding with loved ones, living through the bad times make the good times better.

Not even the devil can make you down! Why? A teaspoon of ice cream is better than a bucket! One small taste and you crave more. If you get a bucket and you feel sick – a little treat although a day of pain – it is why we keep going, each day feeling the devil behind you. Stand strong, do not run, for the day you can turn around and stare him down is the day you win. Live for the pain, learn to love life for each little indifference. Bring on the pain because once you live with it each day not even the devil can make you down.

Try to make the most of each day as if it were your last – you are dead a long time and only live once – make it worth something. Our DNA defines us, our life confines us and our brains imagine most things… I'm a prisoner in my own mind, my body trapped by paralysis, my mind is therefore given time to think… It can be a dangerous thing, chasing your thoughts 24 hrs a day. A strong mind is needed to channel those thoughts down the right route for a life to live, one nearly lost, but brought back from the brink to live again… Life is pain, death is peace – only you can make it worth something.

Hope is the structure of which all life is built, without it we are nothing… With it we can do anything and BE anything. Be who you are, or who you are means nothing.

TODAY

Today is another day given to you to live as you wish to turn your bad luck around and push those boundaries… If you hit a wall, that's fine and understandable – sit and recoup, stand yourself up and try again. Life doesn't just happen; you need to make things happen… 'There is no fate but what we make' and all that. If it doesn't work, push, push and push again. It could all be in vain if we do not make differences and miracles happen in terms of pushing boundaries with manufacturing new equipment and discovering new medication, etc.

Life finds a way… A day like today, will never be here again. Waste it if you wish but there will be no other. There will be another but not that day… it's gone forever.

You'll never be this young again.

I am very lucky to be alive as at one point there was only a 5% chance of me surviving although I was brought back to life. I'm yet to start 'living'; there is a big difference between living and just 'being'. For 13 years I've been a 'human being'. I need to be a 'human living' – to truly live a life nearly taken!

Money has stopped my recovery, I just sit watching what's left waste away. I take a vitamin supplement but that's about it. Spending my days waiting for the next to come. In the past someone once told me, "You have magic hands, you can build anything." Now I have to type using my thumb as my hands no longer work! My fingers are paralysed. I am like a quadruped, although at least dogs can lick their balls! Perhaps I did have magic hands, now that magic fades, but my mind still ticks away, all day, every day – I still have a life to live. If I can build this book with my thumb, who knows where the rest of my body will take me?

A miracle that may never come. I AM more than this… I WILL be more than this… I just need to rescue what is left of me and mould it into what I want me to be!

Tick tock.

Walking through the corridors of life, breathing every breath that I take, the walls around me… the body surrounding me. To what end? I survived such a big thing that could kill most people, pulled through one of the worst things that can happen to a person, not only affecting me, but also changed my life for many of those around me… 13 years!

Thinking about… waiting for… saving for... living for tomorrow.

Today is yesterday's tomorrow; what are you doing more than yesterday? Yesterday's dreams being achieved today?

Nope!

To breathe a breath of freedom, trapped in my own world of paralysis, reflecting each day on those that have passed… Waiting for what may never be – my world.

As I have said, there are pluses: Never underestimate the true value of your health and independence!

Me…

An empty space yet to fill, a day to complete everything I ever wanted to do as your last day is so precious to you… So, why not this one? Today I'm stuck being charged. Running a charge into another set of dead batteries. Inanimate objects dictating my every day. Without these I'd be in bed.

Money...

Money turns the world around. Money creates my world... As I sit here in a broken chair, reliant on everyone for everything – wasting the air that I breathe, it seems! Everybody needs purpose in their lives until the last breath is taken from you... These days are wasted. Unless you act on your dreams they fade away with each day! If you have money for this then it certainly helps. A bomb disposal robot is the technology that'd be on my wish list. Why? It was an idea of mine to use one as a carer in re-using current technology in a different way; an 'out there' idea for independence for transfers and dressing. But with a price tag of £30,000 it is too expensive to buy or even try without certainty, but at a one-off cost at half the price of care in just one year, it could be worth it. (I would possibly need it for 40 more years though, unless COVID-19 finds its way here first).

Life...

Although I still get beaten down every day, somehow I'm still here! Pain is, after all, only telling you you're still alive... it's my life still to live! Frustration equals patience... Through all the hurt you learn to appreciate the quiet times, the calm after the rain, only to find out you're sitting in the eye of the storm. Hold tight, breathe and continue.

Pressure...

The pain... the problems I face...

Still each morning I wake thinking of my future I'm yet to make; yesterday I was Alexander Thomas Smith... Die now and my life is wasted. I need to continue to be that man my mind has made. Today, tomorrow, I am alexwillwalkagain.

My mind is more powerful than my body ever was (still

trying to move a broken body). Spring's here and the ladybugs are out!

Holding on...

Every day slips away... Every day I hold onto what once was, frustrated thinking about what could be, what might be... what should be.

Pain is an interesting thing... I take it, I live it... It becomes what drives me each day. Give up – give in. Take sedation, be nice and relaxed, tucked up in bed away from all the pain.

Nope, not me. The pain and frustration stays with me each day, all day, every day. Each second I feel pain and aches through my body. They stay. Take them from me only for me to become a zombie! Living, breathing but unable to do anything useful... or take the pain and live the frustration only to live another day waiting for what might never be.

A different type of pain today – frustration waiting for my catheter to be changed.

I find myself thinking I am trapped in my mind, trapped within a body broken, trapped inside a house, trapped in a garden, trapped in life! I'm only ever able to do as others dictate – in my chair at 12 noon, back in bed by 5pm, toilet every other day, living in the same place staring through each night at the same ceiling, same walls! My body is in a constant state of survival, rather than relaxed and in recovery. To change yourself, you need to first change your environment, your routine and your outlook on life. Start small and soon great things will come.

I don't feel like that right now though – I give up in this present moment in time with nothing going for me... slowly going backward, losing hope every day, looking down. Every day the same – never anything good coming my way.

People say nothing can get worse, but then... I had a trip

to Stoke Mandeville Hospital, 3 hrs strapped uncomfortably in the back of a transit van, bumping along on my haemorrhoids only to be told I have a kidney stone! Yes, every day can get even worse. I don't have the battery power to walk Dexter, my dog. More pain and discomfort destroying me each day.

Another way to look at it…

BRING ON THE PAIN!

You haven't broken me yet (although my body's broken, my soul still shines). Every day there are new things to deal with; although death has come once for me… I'm still here.

I lost my bed, along with it my last 'comfort zone'… I dropped my slide board transfers and rarely did any standing. I maintained 'skeleton exercise' (my FES bike), I gained weight and lost enthusiasm to do anything, not seeing where I was going.

Thoughts of, I should give up, I should give in and Why don't I use antidepressants? are at the forefront of my mind among a million other thoughts every second of the day, oh, and through the night. Nothing to do, nowhere to go, all avenues used up, unable to do anything!

"This is you now; go home and get on with it," and, "He's just going to have to learn to deal with the pain." I was told that over and over again.

MORE POSITIVE

Yesterday, the same guy repeated this to me, while testing my reflexes in my knees to find nothing ->

Written on my back (in tattoo): Everything comes from nothing – Stephen Hawkins.

Eight years on, I now have perfect reflexes back again! This, along with many other things I have achieved, although still no money/job/love in my life… I have the knowledge that through everything I still have not been broken!

My three-point plan this year is to spend it on getting fit by doing more exercise and bringing back the slide board transfers, to stand up and to go on my bike.

Yesterday, if 'negatives' can turn their view around, I think I can listen to them for once in eight years.

Continue and don't give up!

I'm not going to let the function that I have regained slip away, for every breath I take I will continue! Where I have been, I cannot return… the future… our future… My future is yet to be written; don't write yourself off!

It's not over… I'm not over!

You need to build on who you are now, who you want to be and to never forget the past, where you've been, who you were and what you see now…

Hit rock bottom!

At some stage in all our lives, even for those of course who are able-bodied, we feel we've hit 'rock bottom'. At every point in life, no matter how low, there is always a light on somewhere. Even if it's not quite pointing your way, when there's nothing else, dig a little hole! There's always another option.

One day, everything was looking down for me. I couldn't take any more. I broke down thinking that nothing could get worse, then the following morning I discovered my catheter tube had come apart in the night and I woke up in a bed full of urine! My iPad and TV remote were swimming. This set the day on a downer as you can imagine. After the cold of the short January days and being in bed by 5pm (a bed without comfort, hypersensitivity removing any bed mobility), I went into the evening thinking, What's next? Nothing can be worse and Can't take any more when my catheter blocks for the third time that month – extreme pain and autonomic dysreflexia (AD) – danger of death. All this on top of the fact I can't move!

Today, however, is another day… I'm not dead, so I feel I need to do something with it!

Spring is here! So when you're feeling down you can smile and think of me knowing that 'life isn't that bad'.

TURNING LIFE AROUND

Let's look at the facts:

I drowned… I survived.

I broke my neck… I survived.

My heart stopped six times… I still live.

My lungs gave up… I still breathe.

Life goes on, inside and around me… even if surviving is all I do.

To function in life, we all need purpose.

Is surviving different to living life? I think so.

Pain is an ice cube…. Visualise it as this and focus on it… Watch it melt away to minimise the physical state of pain… Relief in the mind reduces physical pain, allowing yourself time to think how to resolve the rest of it.

Without time, we do not exist… I've learnt time, I live time… I've learnt patience, I am patience. We are energy – signals shot from one neuron to another. I live only through pathways built inside me and the routes they take govern me. Be everything you are, be all you can be. Push those limits, open that door to everything inside you. The one truth in life… you are who you are and nothing/no one can change that. If the pathways are blocked today they can be re-built tomorrow.

For now, my body is being maintained by functional electrical stimulation directly into my muscles via my bike; this bypasses the blockage in my neck.

Open up your mind to the world around you, open the door to who you are, break down everything only to be built back up. I am broken temporarily but I will be re-built!

Today, my teeth… tomorrow, who knows?

Before breaking my neck (roughly eight weeks prior, about 8½ years ago) I was planting 160 trees, all needing wooden stakes. I was hitting them in with a post rammer and I hit one too hard, bouncing the tool up. Still pulling it down I brought it straight down onto my head, splitting it open (3 cms needed gluing back together). The resulting force made my bottom jaw hit the top, knocking out my front tooth! I had a temporary bridge fitted for 5½ months. I went away to work (October–February) to return home to get the finished work done. This all changed December 14th when I broke my neck… So today's the day I get the rest of the dental work done, 8½ years later.

If you don't accept one day you will die you may never actually have lived – we all break. Not all of us can be fixed!

Everything came from nothing – Stephen Hawkins.

It can take a lifetime to come to terms with some things. (TV advert)

1, 2, 3, 4, 5, 6… breathe!

Believe in who you want to be – adapt, evolve and continue!

I am nothing, own nothing; can't do anything…

TRUTH AND REALITY

I can be anything as everything comes from nothing, it's just depressing and soul-destroying always starting over. Unlike others looking in job centres or avoiding them in a lot of cases, I start from being unable to even manoeuvre, get out of bed or unable to sit up correctly in a profiling bed (hinges at my ribs instead of waist). Two days in from being kicked square in the balls yet again through sheer frustration and a little thought process (from hours uncomfortably awake), I can now sit up/ pull myself up (using a rope ladder, bed mechanism and side bars), even though being knocked back, I bounce back quick. I don't bounce in the literal sense, I still hit the floor like a sack of $#|+.

Even my plants were all dying, but by clearing out the dead ones I found that four mango trees and my pineapple tree are growing.

There has to be some reason that I didn't die that day. A lot of people worked hard to bring me back, so… right now, today, I feel happy with basic bed mobility and another blank slate to try.

Lose everything, have nothing but to regain a lust for living…

IMAGININGS

Belief in the seemingly impossible…

My mind is struggling to deal with being forced backwards at every turn. I am finding things difficult right now (this whole year). I don't know how to say this politely but you get to a 'Fuck walking, I just want my independence' stage.

I haven't been on my bike or much else productive these past few weeks. Frustration is my best friend now. It's when you get to that part of the day when everything is going wrong, you think, I know, I feel like being strapped onto a machine and electrocuted for two hours! (my bike).

The night before last was like being brought back seven years, unable to do anything at all. Last night I slept like the dead (a good night!)

My bed was designed for the elderly and infirm, the paralysed and the bedridden. I looked at it this morning once HOISTING out (slide board transfers [out], not possible due to design). My body bends at the hip as I'm sure does every other human's on this planet! Why then does my bed hinge at the point of my ribs, pushing me down every time it is up, with no way of being able to push myself up?

This takes out most bed mobility, then the side (baby

bars) get taken down to 'get out of bed' (hoist/slide/or fall!) I need these to hook my gimpy arms through. To turn alone is impossible being paralysed from the nipples down! I utilise what I have to do what I need.

I have to remind myself that I have achieved a lot – making the impossible possible over these past few years, waiting for everything – EVERYTHING! And saying thank you for everything all day long for everything all the time, even down to inserting suppositories and then proceeding to 'stimulate' my bowel ('digital stimulation'). The first time I actually cried was in Miami. Transferring from ICU after two days into rehab, I knew things were serious (being paralysed) as I just thought, 4–6 months, maybe a year and then back to work, back to my life… Nope! A video on bowel management and 'this is you, now' is what I went through… So if you're reading this and you're interested (sorry) – a finger in your butt and then thanking the person!?

Before that would result in fighting talk (polite version!)

EXPENSES

All summer I've been without my boma chair due to the most expensive part breaking at a cost of £240. The complete chair costs a little over £10,000! Those two parts, a seat and four wheels attached to a frame, how do you get to 10,000? By the way, the cushion is £375 extra – that isn't even the expensive one (which is a j2 cushion).

All my stuff is extremely over-priced. They're not one-off buys either! I'm not getting up and about any time soon, it was eight years December just gone since I received some of my equipment! Everything has been bought and mostly funded by the very generous Holland America Line and helped in kind, money and time by my family and friends – THANK YOU.

Thank you for your time and your support.

I need extremely over-priced things every day, all day. People can't and don't want to keep supplying and giving/fundraising; everybody gets tired at some point or there is another good cause that comes along to raise funds for. I am going to need things throughout the duration of my life. They're not toys but tools just to have a good night's sleep or to 'walk' the dog, which are beneficial!

As well as equipment I have to have care – people in and out for weeks at a time. It's all very personal, no social boundaries with strangers in and out constantly. I have even looked at equipment that is already out there but to use it in a different way – it could be for my independence, a robotic platform with robotic arm and webcam that I could possibly operate (using my iPad), to dress myself and very possibly use it to transfer (the act of transferring from one bed to another or to and from a piece of equipment, etc). As with other things these are not exact but you can only find out if you try.

There are other units out there, but just using the same technology in a slightly different way. Again, these things are expensive and at the risk of failure, so at present a no-go, but with this current pandemic evolving (see more in Epilogue), last year, for me, a cold turned to pneumonia and a hospital trip lead to a pressure sore resulting in becoming bedridden for 3½ months!

CONTINUING ON – AGAIN

I am paralysed, I am continuing… I am alexwillwalkagain.

Yet another example – the night before last showed me how frustrating my life can be. Giving up is not an option – my main goal is to live alone with my dog, living independently – not needing to beg or grovel for anything. I need to be the man I was born to be, not a pathetic waste of time and space that I see myself becoming… It's a fight every day for who I am on the inside.

Breathe – I can only continue or die trying.

True beauty is something that you will never see. Open your eyes to the world around you. It is only something you find within yourself. Feel it, then you will see what you're looking for.

Life itself, when it's running out… it's the most precious thing to anyone. One more day, please? Sorry, too late!

Live your life the way you want, you never know when it will be taken from you. Your lifeblood and yours alone goes through that heart in that chest of yours!

At the point of injury my body wouldn't give up, I pulled through the unimaginable. Every day since I have lived with very little ability to do anything, needing help for everything, awake through each night, unable to sleep. Not only am I paralysed, I get all the little extra repercussions that come with it! Lack of function, sensations all twisted up, hot when cold, hurting when nothing's wrong. A feather touch burns like fire, cold water burns. Having to electrocute myself four times a week for 54-minute sessions, just to maintain the little function I do have!

Myself an inspiration? I can't see this. Give up or go on!

Hitting a wall that I can't get past, my mind stays strong and, someway pushing through, I don't know how and find myself lying awake at 02:19 hrs writing things down purely to clear my head.

Where is life taking me? Who knows?

POSITIVITY

Trying not to take life too serious... but even peeing has to be done through my stomach! Most days I'm getting through by liquid going in and coming out just to keep a pipe from blocking to stop AD. I'm happy to pee myself instead of going through that! (My head trying to split open from the inside just because I can't pee, or just to tell me I'm lying on a fold in the sheet).

Can't you find love? Haven't you got the right handbag to match your shoes? My problems are not as trivial as yours – I don't have these 'problems' but yours are what drive you. This is an insight into my life!

As my blood still flows my heart still pumps. I go on each day – positive as ever. I live and keep going, but what life truly holds for any of us nobody knows.

For now, what I know is keeping me going is, I got this far.

Energy is life.

Every day I wake, feel the energy. People talk about 'the soul', how the body moves.

Find this guy on YouTube – Bob Ross Remixed – Happy Little Clouds – one of my inspirations to get going in the morning.

To be free of the need to have help with everything, my 'go to' is www.quadtools.com.

WHAT MAKES ME TICK

I ride my bike, roughly 20 miles each time. I plug myself into the mains supply and the bike stimulates the muscles in my legs and bum into cycling. Instead of receiving signals from my brain through the spinal cord it does this via a computer directly into my muscles.

Some days I have very little energy, other days plenty… In December 2006 I flatlined and my energy levels stopped completely on six different occasions. I still had life left to live, however, so here I am in 2020 living life as I can… Pressing, pushing, pulling my way through each day, a reason for everything… A path laid down… A destiny written… Who knows how, when or who by..? I'm definitely not finished… But there are many, many hours each day spent wondering why..? Why me..? Why this path..?

For now I can't change anything, I can only walk the path that I'm on, deal with the cards that I'm dealt. I focus my energy this way, maintaining the way I am, who I am and trying to work out where I am!

Life is all about energy, how we create it, hold onto it and use it. Once the energy is extinguished the life you know is no more.

Alexander Thomas Smith – chained down by my own body – trapped by my own mind.

Riding through the wake of the midnight fire, riding my bike my own way, living my life my own way! I've definitely picked the more difficult way… but that's the result of 'learn from your mistakes'.

Looking for sanctuary, a world I may never see!

Every day pushing… hoping… trying for what many say is the unachievable…

I've already been told:

"This is you now, get on with it!"

"You're living in a fantasy world."

"Why don't you just stay in bed?"

"If I was you…"

That's just it though, you're not me… I AM! I don't even know yet what my body is truly capable of; I'm not stopping until I can find out! No one can tell me any different… They think they can… but my ears don't hear it!

This year so far I've been hit by a chest/throat infection that I'm yet to shake off. The antibiotics finished today and I'm about to start my bike, hoping this can sweat things out! You see, I'm still here and until they take me completely I will push every day.

THE FUTURE

I aim to achieve the impossible!

Watch this space ______________________________

Life is harsh. 'Leave the weak to die' but the weak is me! I'm not ready to go just yet, I fight through the day and sometimes I'm awake through the night. Something inside me is saying "Not today, not just yet!" There's a storm rising inside me. Every day it's building up and one day soon it'll fire up! Fix me or kill me! I'm tired of this game. Some things are just meant to be. This one is 'just me'. I walk this road and ride the pain, I'm pushing through paralysis, pushing it right off the cliff – my life, my way! A voice from the shadows, a voice through the night, I am but a whisper… The echo of what millions of people go through every day. I wake up faced with a solid wall, a wall that might as well be as thick as the ground itself with no way through to the other side.

Seven years have passed since I woke from my coma, from near-death. I was six times defibrillated (resuscitated) to be alive again! For this I thank you, my family and friends who stuck by me in Miami and to Holland America Line. I live a life of pain, frustration and forced patience. Through all this I still hold onto hope, a spark inside that may one day light the fire that will burn through the ground itself! The planet we stand on has a molten core, a fire inside – this is me. Every day I dig away at the surface, hoping to find the thing that may cure me.

It IS POSSIBLE for me to one day walk again! Every day I push for a little more – an independent life.

No one can say what is coming next. All you can do is wait. Be prepared for what might be – anything CAN BE, for you or for me, life may be a prison. But one thing that it is, it's your life. I was given this life back, you have yours, live the day like it's your own. Be who you are. I am Alexander Thomas Smith, living paralysed every day, free in my mind, free in my dreams, yet stuck only by my body. I dream of: independence… positivity… recovery… happiness… success… It doesn't have to be in that order, the order changes daily. For me my independence ranks very high; it's what keeps me heading in the right direction. A lot of people like to create the illusion of success when in reality they are riding the opposite wave.

One thing about my situation is everything is out there for you to see, for everybody measures success differently. Your decisions in life help to define who you are, so do the mistakes… but LEARN from them. We wouldn't be human after all if we didn't allow ourselves a mistake or two. Mine just happened to be a rather large mistake. All you can do is to ensure you learn and adapt each time. I'm nearly seven years paralysed! As you can imagine, my outlook changed on life incredibly after hitting my head, which lead on to a series of catastrophic events.

Each day is one day closer to death but each day is closer to a cure – as I said earlier, live it like it's your last! As you grow up you're moulded by the events and experiences that take place as time rolls on, some good things and some bad.

Ultimately, do what makes YOU happy. I'm a happy bunny today. My mistakes, myself to blame – me.

The life I once lived wasn't all that great… The life I have now isn't what I want… but this life is the one I own! It is what leads me to who I will be. If you're with me you will see that in time you will see a new future unfold! Stand for what you believe in, stand for what you want. My days are long but I've learned to wait every day.

Only what might be – Alexwillwalkagain!

I may be stuck inside a broken body but my mind is still alive – it is 01:15 hrs as I type this. Throughout my life I have always risen back up after being kicked down, but this time I seem to be rolling back down the hill. I will stand on my own two feet again. I strive for what I had – good health, fitness and independence. I do like material things and you can make your life more special by surrounding yourself with shiny things that give you happiness. It's in our nature to hunt and collect, but my ultimate goal is for independence, to be alone, live alone and walk alone! Care and attention day in and day out, though required and wished for by the elderly is not what I want any more – it can make your butt a bit raw!

Hold onto the good things in your life for a moment because, although you may be living a life like mine, the simple things in life can give the most pleasure. Life passes you by before you know it. I cannot turn back the clock or change my past.

I love my fluffy man, Dexter! Today my two-year-old niece, Bethany, and I were admiring a picture of Tyler, my late Staffy (RIP 24/08/2010 x). She said, "Poor Tyler puppy. You'll never be back again," and then turned to Dexter and said, "If you weren't born, Tyler would come back!" Children have an uncanny way of telling things straight. The time I had with

Tyler is worth more money than all the world has as he got me through so much. I will never let his memory go, but now it's Dexter's time! He gives me much pleasure. Good times to come, but live for what is now. I can't walk, I can't stand and I can't even sit up… but, fuck it! Live life for now, not for what's next or what has been! Have I made that message clear enough now?

For just over a year I've been sitting on a plateau… I had physio today with Steve, standing with stability in my chair with the parallel bars. Today was my best standing yet! I may have just improved from 'maintaining' to 'improving'. Today went well and I'll continue with my FES bike and standing up and in eight weeks we'll see if there's more to say. A girl once said to me "Think positive and don't dwell on the past." So, don't sit worrying about what's happened, instead use that negative energy to make your future better. Just don't hide away from all the hurt! If you survive you come out the other side stronger.

Every day is like a movie – the film reel runs out before you realise – 'blink and it's gone'. Sometimes you run the wrong film reel in your mind and sometimes it's a repeat… You could look back and see the re-runs in your mind, but unlike a movie there are no re-takes. Change things now in the present so when you're looking back in the future you can see you made the right choices now.

Through the heat there are always methods to cool down, but in the cold? It is harder to get warm but if you look you will find heat. I have found its energy; if you feel it in your heart you can achieve it – 'life finds a way'. After this positive thinking, however, my positivity took a hit these past few days. I have been in bed today under a fan by 15:30 hrs! The sun's out… maybe for a week, or a month… Also, I have the frustration of the fact I haven't been on my bike today, although I have done 6974 miles to date! I have been determined to maintain my health and fitness through six long years and, even though I have been down today, I'll be back tomorrow. I know I will never get my old self back but each day I work on my new self.

Even though I have dissolved scar tissue and a reduction in the size of my cyst there is no removal of the titanium neck plate or screws to be had or the second-hand C6 vertebra. I still have a lot to get through, but I've been through so much already, I'm not stopping just yet. I've proven to be… me!

My life is slow this week, I have been out in the fresh air most of today only to return to a very rude reception. I was brought up to respect other people, especially when entering someone's house to remove one's shoes, etc. I'll give you an example: one person recently came into my life that was paid to assist me in my independence. Although competent in many aspects of the job (my life), the one way to describe her is R.U.D.E! Previously, I had a lovely PA doing the same job (again, my life), whereas the entire assignment felt like just two days whereas the other one was hard work at only two days in! I know this Monday can't come quick enough! It feels like a month has passed…

carer *noun* the person who has the responsibility for looking after an ill, disabled or otherwise dependent person.

As you can see, the description does not cover rude, self-centred or lazy! To be 'a carer', it should state 'to be like Lucie!' Just thought I'd tell anyone who's listening…

People come, people go… Everyone lives their lives, some people stay and some are not that important! Some come into your life quietly but make the biggest impact. That could be a dog, cat or shark, even a honey-eating bunny! I will take my kite to the beach, show Dexter the sea. I will swim in a shark tank and feed some big cats.

As I write the wind's blowing up outside, like the sands of time drifting away second by second… My mind inspires me to write, sometimes nothing in particular. Most things on here are a record of my progress through FES and physio. Life changes you… You build your life, so who builds who?

If a bunny gave you a year, what would you do with it? Really, what would you do? I'm starting with lions…

POSITIVITY – AGAIN

I started the year negatively, now I'm pushing to be positive! A new thing each week… not too much… Just a change here and there, as hard as life can be… When one day ends another begins.

Through my eyes Bruce Lee influences my strength.

Through everything I still have choice. I was thinking this year was bad… It's not bad-bad, things happen, but it's down to me, how I live. Even though I am broken, I still wake each day – a new day! I can be told something 1000 times but I am the one who chooses when to listen, when to act! My thoughts run my life, being as I am, stuck in a crazy mind pinned down by paralysis.

A few years back I started writing. I may stop tomorrow or I might keep going for another 50 years, it's like Forrest Gump and his running. I know I have to maintain what I have achieved so far and keep up on my bike. Realisation today says I am the only one who can stop myself – only I truly know what my body can do. Even without physical function I still have mental function.

Me, myself and I!

Since my autonomic episodes (high blood pressure, sit/

stand up), all the problems I have been through these past few weeks I think are just after-effects from this. For instance, I was in the shower yesterday listening to music (little Dexter sleeps on a towel in the corner of the bathroom while I do this). My left side went tingly then numb before I proceeded to faint. I called out but through the music I was muffled... Dexter woke and started barking until the carer came to my rescue! Thank you, Dexter. Already he's earning his breakfast. When fainting, my blood pressure means low (LOW, raise legs/lay down). Others may differ. Since yesterday morning this numb feeling has returned three times.

All different scenarios...

Left hand, little finger to index, left leg. My sensation changes from time to time; I believe AD has brought on some changes. It's classed as a medical emergency as mentioned earlier. I'm normally full of nerve pain in the above mentioned parts (a harsh sunburn, for instance) so I don't know if it's good or bad yet. I called Stoke Mandeville for confirmation on my theory but unfortunately, as with many other phone calls, there was no real progress achieved. I keep reminding myself, however, that after coming home for the first time I only had movement in my neck, having just 54% sensation throughout my body. Over time with perseverance and through physio, I have regained 90% of this sensation (using a technique with cotton wool and a sharp pin). Hot and cold feelings have also returned (as I mentioned earlier, but sometimes they're in reverse), along with the ability – very recently – to sweat! I now also have much more motor function throughout. Another bonus is that, prior to this I was kept indoors above 20° Celsius and now I can sit in the sun! (At the time of writing the UK is experiencing a glorious spell of weather, so this means a lot).

As I have alluded to many times, I still find myself

questioning from time to time, why? In ICU Miami that Christmas night, both the guy next to me and I flatlined… They got me back but he died… What would he be doing if the situation were the other way round? 'Why I should rise and you should not' – quote from a song, The Walking Dead, Series 3… Some songs jar memories from time to time; that one just hit home to me – life, hope and positivity.

I died six years ago! But they brought me back, not once, but six times!

If life pushes you… push back.

It's true only the strong survive! My body is still numb from AD today and my head still hurts. Any little movement brings on the start-up symptoms of AD; I believe this will calm overnight.

Paralysis is hard every minute… Paralysis is a real shit! Every day, to look from the outside in.

I don't feel I am an inspiration. I am in a downward spiral and no matter what happens, the life that I live right now keeps going. Sometimes it makes me feel pathetic and useless, reliant on everyone for everything… and the catheter site on my stomach is red raw.

The one thing I do have is that my mind is alive in a broken body. My mind is alive and does not actually require any assistance to think; I'm trapped by my own thoughts.

Today I received another piece to the puzzle that is the Quinn family, spread throughout the globe – this time from Australia! We are definitely flung far and wide but truly from strong blood! Through times of hardship and heartache we are always family. The support I have around me drives my need to succeed although it may not come across at times. The puzzle I am referring to is a large picture of family members that my wider family circle has contributed to. Bit by bit I receive pieces in the post and they are very welcomed by me. I would love to mention my less immediate family by name but I have around 60 first cousins! It is comforting to know that family are thinking of me and care enough.

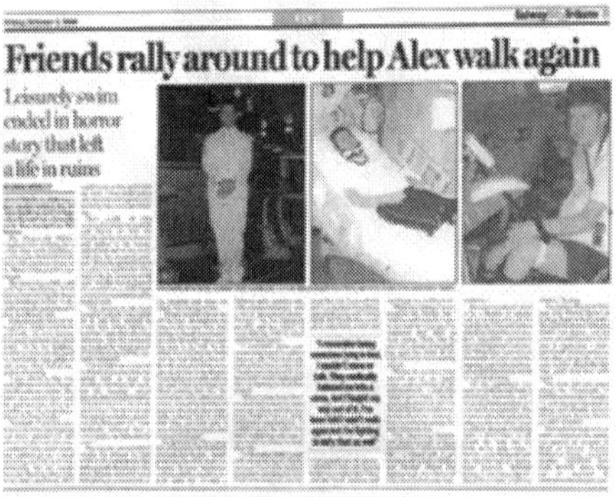
Friends rally around to help Alex walk again

Leisurely swim ended in horror story that left a life in ruins

This is a local newspaper article [entitled 'Friends rally around...' which is self-explanatory. I owe a lot to friends and family

A life spent with me... A life spent watching me... A life spent without me... Either way it's a life spent! Never to be again. Each one is yours, use it doing what makes you happy for, as I keep reminding you, you never know what tomorrow holds.

In one lifetime it's possible to live 1000 different ways...

The choices you make may not always be yours or the right ones, but it's only you that is walking that road. 'You're born alone, you die alone'. What you do in-between, who you're doing it with, that comes down to you – good or bad – whatever happens you're the one living it! You decide – your life. 'The only thing we HAVE to do is die'. Do something, please, either alone or with that someone, do it before you can't! Right now it's Chuck and me... It's easier to type than to do.

Remember, 1000 paths to walk…

My heart still beats… I still have things to do… Even though I may only be rolling here, I came back a little broken… but I still did it!

Sometimes you just need to say "Bollocks!"

In life you need to stand your ground, if you fight and lose… One day maybe, they may find my cure, but until then, bring on the same, the same every day, bring on what you can! I'm here waiting. One day perhaps alexwillwalkagain.

All my problems are logged on here! It is therapeutic for me to get them all down on paper. There is nothing for me today other than a walk with Chuck. Tomorrow I strap my 'dead' legs onto my FES bike for another 20ish miles.

Bring on tomorrow's tomorrow… Nobody knows what will be… I don't even know where I'm going with this paragraph!? Tomorrow will be today in an hour and a half. I might know more other than Chuck's doing well pooping outside. He's just a bit confused about where to pee…

Talk hard, follow your heart; it may not be clear where life is leading you but each day the mist does clear a little. Draw strength from that where you can – only you can decide what you do with the life you live (and hopefully, love)…

I keep turning the pages in time… It slips away too fast, the story of life changes every day. Each time you blink, each breath you breathe, life moves on with or without you. Six times I've left but they put the air right back in my lungs and I'm still here doing seemingly nothing with it. You then look back and right here I have written down where I've been and what I've done these past six years. I am what is inside your heart… blood and pressure, energy and aura. It's the lifeblood of all of us; I am broken, I may never be fixed, but inside I maintain strength and positivity through everything. I cannot give you an answer why, I just do. I've tried letting go and giving in and I just can't – not yet – and I don't think I could ever reach that point... Some of the random thoughts going through my head: my life... walking... independence... love... staying strong and keeping it going. Keep pushing through the pain and flog that dead horse – mine has defibrillators attached, it's been flogged so much... Money... Survival or living... Take today... Too tired to bike... Too worn out to transfer... Raining on and off, living and breathing but nothing doing. A day I'd want back later on, perhaps? But for now it's gone. I will maintain my health and fitness, just had to lose today! I'll try again tomorrow – life.

Free will has consequence, sometimes take a moment to think before you act – I'm stuck thinking a thousand thoughts every day, unable to move! I will maintain, while medical research continues... I have to wait but I think life is lived in-between any plans made...

It can't rain all the time – Brandon Lee, The Crow.

CONNECTIONS

Everything is connected in this world, everything is connected within us! My body works... I just have a cyst, scar tissue, some screws and a titanium plate blocking my connections within my neck. My will is strong but I can say it wavers from time to time...

Of course, I will maintain my health, fitness and complete physical wellbeing hoping for what may never come... Living with what functions I do have... Maintaining things for anything that may be... Hoping to jolt something within me, to create that connection that helps me move.

Everyone seems to want what they cannot have, from a girl wishing for all the riches in the world and people say, "At least you have your health." I never thought there was 'wealth' in that – I spent nine months in a caravan! All I had was my health (and baby Tyler!) Now look at what I've done to myself! My 'recovery' may stretch over years. I'm fully aware I'll never be as I was, I just want my independence. The tech is here and available and over these past few years I've definitely been a thinker instead of a doer. Perhaps that will change... maybe not... Only time will tell.

Money does help! But health is everything. Tomorrow –

standing, then Monday – bike (another 20 miles to nowhere) maintaining what I have, hoping for what might come; who knows?

Everybody dies... Not everyone truly lives.

As stated earlier, I was unlucky enough for my expensive chair to break. While opening my eyes to the whole 'waiting for everything', so many things were building up inside, I felt like I needed to explode. Instead of thinking what would have, could have or might have been I need to work with what I have while waiting for all those plans to show themselves. So even though I'm wide awake at midnight, I believe I have enough resources about to fit 'my spec chair' together.

From nine months of the comfiest time in the womb, to the first journey home, to leaving home to find your way... Even waking up in hospital with a priest standing over you waiting for him to start the last rites... I did ask him to leave – I wasn't going then and I'm still not ready yet! It's frustrating waiting patiently for an itch to disappear because you are unable to scratch it yourself. It's frustrating feeling your chest change temperature as your lungs fill with fluid until the man comes along to hoover you out through the hole in your neck. I'm not too sure what I spent today waiting for, but I know I'm not doing the same tomorrow! (Mid-text, there were just a few memories from hospital).

Life is gone in a moment... there are no limitations... no restrictions... but altogether, everything all at once, life is fragile and harder than rock. Do something to be remembered by and leave a legacy or choose to fade into time. At the moment I am all I can be but not all I'm going to be. Life changes you and moulds you into everything you are.

I'm alive... but I'll be a long time dead.

This world's not quite finished with me yet. Bring on

all that may come… Adapt, don't accept! Life happens, you choose the path to walk… I took the wrong one, but my life must mean something as I came back. What that is yet, by the way, I'm yet to find out… It may not be important. It may be I just forgot something yet to do. Those who've passed, you were everything!

I just need to find that something!

REACHING OUT TO OTHERS

Of course, you may be thinking But surely he interacts with others in similar situations so he doesn't feel so alone? I originally had a website through WordPress called www.alexwillwalkagain.com and my life was out there for people to see. Your life… it's private, but I chose to put mine out there. I started a record of my ongoing recovery (at the time I didn't know it would be this ongoing). I've documented roughly four years of my life now – the ins, outs, ups and downs. The main reason being the wider family members could get updates on my progress and people could connect with me throughout the World Wide Web, from Greece to Texas and Rockford, Illinois, all the way down in Mexico. There were people just coming into this world of paralysis – some living, some a little lost (as I found myself throughout). By talking, supporting, sharing and giving advice on personal experiences, we gave each other insights into our lives after injury. The advice included the very basic of needs too – skincare! I was urged to get a mattress and cushion to avoid skin damage. Luckily I have recovered and maintained my muscles well. Sepsis is one of the main worries – the hidden killer coming from infection. Fundraise as you go and equipment can be found.

Apart from having my family members on the social media site with me, which was obviously wonderful to have so much support, there is the other side of the coin. Regarding on-line help groups, sometimes via Facebook or individually, with everyone seeking help and advice, looking for positivity but finding only people crying out and lost without direction, could somewhat feel negative and depressing. Everyone in this world, from whichever background, with or without paralysis, have struggles and worries. We have problems that seem huge, but we each have our ways to deal with things, right or wrong. I found that, sometimes, the on-line communication was no longer a comfort. This is where the book fits, a guide to how I have lived my life from the point of injury to the present day. I still lose myself each day – it only matters when you can't find your way back again. Everyone struggles through life at times; there are no handbooks on how to do it (that's why I wrote one!)

The other reason for this book is that my on-line diary blog got hacked, cleaned up and then, six months later due to a backdoor programme being installed by them, it was hacked again and destroyed! They had posted some very malicious things on there too. Recovering most of the real information, I created this handbook instead. As a book I figured that it couldn't get hacked. It's just another example of one road blocked in life leading onto something possibly bigger and better. Until your story ends, nobody knows.

L.I.F.E.

All my disappointments are born from the situation I created the day for myself that I broke my neck! All those sayings of encouragement I have mentioned previously: 'Don't live in the past', 'Love yourself' and 'You can't change what's happened' – BOLLOCKS! Fuck it! YOU try living as I am with what I have and try to accept it! No independence every day, to be in a prison… Sometimes I feel helpless but never have I felt free! For five years I have fought to walk again. I fight for, over everything, my independence!

THANK YOUS

Apart from the companies I mentioned earlier, I also say thanks to the wonderful people who drink in Drakes in Maidstone, you have propelled me forward to my main goal right now – my goal for independence. You raised the money for me to buy: right and left mini arms, a long reach right arm and a left knife arm, bringing the hope for independence that little bit closer – thank you! I know right now I'm living on a plateau as regards to recovery as they are researching a cure. I'm never giving up the hope for my independence and one day walking again; until then, creating a semi-independent life however I can, is the best I can do. Some people have said I'm an inspiration… I don't think it's me that can take the credit, it's everyone around me; I just have to keep going somehow. Every day things happen that people live through. This just takes a bit of patience.

I got an envelope today from New York, it said 'Once you reach the end of the rope, tie a knot in it and hold on'. So true for my situation right now! I am definitely riding a plateau, maintaining my health and fitness and most of all, my sanity!

JELLYFISH

I think that they may have broken me to sit back and contemplate life!

Two hours being electrocuted can make your mind wander… I broke my neck at C5/C6; this is 'incomplete' so restricts signals from my brain to body. This does tend to piss me off most days. My legs are still fully functional – even after five long, long years just waiting for medical science to catch up with me.

Here's the technical bit… A jellyfish has no brain! But some have eyes… They don't think, they just do! They can process colour, shapes, light and dark… but with what? Spinal reflex is something we use to function on a daily basis, eg, when walking you're not thinking, Left leg, right leg over and over… You're more likely thinking, Not more work… or I need to pee... maybe, or What's in the fridge? then your legs just do the work! Spinal reflex! This is a kind of simple example of how I ride the FES bike, but using electric pulses directly to the muscles to keep things working. I need someone out there to bypass the point of injury, via a bridge using a metal strip or similar implant. By using a similar FES computer that my brain can send signals to, the signals 'jump' the point of injury using the implanted bridge, allowing my body to function, or from my brain to the computer to my muscles. I use a suit with wires to bypass if I can ride a bike using this technology. It can't be impossible to restore function so I can have my body back…

I'm slowly, slowly imploding in on myself… To give up still isn't me; my body functions just not as it did! I carry 70% of me. Laying still my body is on fire, nerve pain throughout… Drugs calm this, as does exercise. My FES bike helps maintain and calm down my body in case, in case, in case new things happen!

Tread slowly if you ever find yourself in a croc pit.

We all need a voice as our lives are short in this world. Since chalk was put to wall, quill to bark and pen to paper, now I'm communicating to you via my thumb to iPad; the written word in this digital world is spread at the touch of a button worldwide… My voice may help you or it may not! Either way it's out there now; my life, my mistakes, my experiences, my day. Your day will soon be tomorrow, tomorrow will become today… Blink, then the next day will be gone too. Remember to live your life how you want, be what you want.

This… this is me!

Life is fragile… With today's technology and the advances in medical science, nobody can say what will happen tomorrow… The Incas thought the world would end in 2012. I'm going to continue maintaining my health, fitness, mobility and hope for independence in the years to follow. As with everybody restricted by money and time, and at the time of writing, the lockdown, time slips away and in need of a mountain of money but never getting further than an ant hill!

Nerve pain is my brain talking to my muscles through the 'incomplete' pathways and tangled mess of undirected regenerated ones. I feel pain. I feel both light and deep sensation down through 77% of my body – sensation over motor function and, down the left side, hyper-sensation and prolonged, delayed, intense sensation.

The research is in progress, but I live as I am the best way that I see I can. There will always be ways to live better but it's my heart that leads me… It's not what others see but what I see, what I feel that I am. I've made a mess of the body that I was born into but built my mind to be strong.

FROM EARLY YEARS AND CAREER... TO WHERE I AM NOW

I was born in the UK into a family of six. My dad's British and my mum's Irish. My dad's one of two siblings, my mum's one of 19, hence the 60 first cousins I mentioned earlier! This brings our bloodline way across the globe from Galway to Australia, across the USA and back. My four siblings are Elliot, myself, Ross and Jennifer.

At two years old the family moved to Zambia for four years as my dad's job took us out there as an engineer on the copper mines. We returned to the UK in time for my seventh birthday, to Staplehurst in Kent, until I reached 17 where I moved to South Shields near Newcastle to train as a marine engineer. I returned home 3½ years later as a fully qualified engineer and Officer in the British Merchant Navy, working for a further three years for P&O Ferries. I then chose to try working ashore for another three years, but nothing really worked out, so I found my way back to sea, very nearly going onto luxury yachts. I chased the cruise ship route and found myself travelling to join the MS Westerdam in Alaska for four months. This lead onto a very short but intense ride, until breaking my neck on December 14th 2006.

Fire training at South Tyneside College, Newcastle – class 7ns1, C.2000 (I'm second from right)

Me with MS Westerdam behind me

Very proud, wearing my crew uniform as a fully qualified Officer, on the MS Westerdam in Alaska, C.2006

My life has been full of adventures... Growing up I set fire a few times to the field using petrol, then drove through the wall of flames on a motorbike that also had a fuel leak. I was tied by my feet to the back of a car and dragged round at about 30mph. This lead onto skiing on my knees behind the car, also jumping from the bike to the car while moving and climbing into the sunroof... I was definitely one for taking risks. Now I'm afraid to transfer from bed to chair – how life changes! A memory of a life once lived.

Another time, my brother, Elliot, ran me over in our field and yes, I've once been held up at gunpoint! When I was only two years old I climbed a fence and a length of wire went into my eye! I'm talking, right in! I have a scar but I can still see. Here I am. All I have to do is walk. I'm sure I can manage that. As you know, I've also cracked my head open three times, smashed my teeth out six times... I've had the bone 'pop' out of my wrist and broken it on another occasion. I am still here and living!

This book holds my voice and the record of my recovery to date, although now I stand still in my recovery. All I did was to go swimming. That choice haunts me every day, but even today I still breathe... I can't walk but I talk hard. I need to live as I type... to know me each day...

Follow me, or don't... it's your choice, one day at a time. I live it as I am.

Read the story of my life to see what happened, see how one choice can mould a life and make your own judgement. I can't keep hold of threads of memories past, I need to weave what I live now into more than just TEXT. I will ride my FES RTI 300 bike again tomorrow, to maintain my health and fitness, lowering fat build-up, helping blood circulation, reducing calcium build-up in my joints, preventing paralysed ligaments seizing up, reducing spasms in my muscles, maintaining bone density and muscle mass. Most of all, keeping my sanity and my heart and lungs strong. I go roughly nine miles each time – insect bites for 54 minutes (the electricity flowing through me!) Nearly 6000 miles to nowhere!

To accept my physical state has obviously been the hardest thing in the world. Every minute of every day I think of ways to live as I am. I will adapt and I will become the man I choose to be. Right now, however, I don't know how to get there, but again, that is my choice to make.

The only thing in life you have to do is die, everything else you decide!

Both in Miami and over here they say recovery is 12–18 months. I've pressed, pushed, bent and beat those boundaries. Five years in and I've only just hit a plateau. I fight every day still (even if it is in my own mind). I am Alexander Thomas Smith and on December 14th 2006, that is when I began the next chapter in my life.

Bad things happen… but sometimes good things can come from them.

A coin,
One coin,
Two coins… all the coins,
Everything, all of it and nothing!

I have a lot to be thankful for – I have my health, I have my bed and I'm fed every day. Happiness can be everything, it can be a single glass of water on a hot day – it's different for every person… It's different every day. Today it was cold and I needed warmth; I may need more tomorrow. The world is a double-sided coin.

To feel your chest heat up from inside with frustration, the knot inside. It takes so long to do anything! There is no outlet for what I feel. Depression, frustration and pain… it's called paralysis.

Winnie (my other little dog, has allergies to everything) has shed her fur. It's re-grown, as she does, every day stronger… Every day I get closer to my independence! I'll fight each day to achieve it. I won't give up. I went through all that I have and my pulse still beats. As my lungs draw each breath I will continue this fight through paralysis. Taking the bad along with the good, one day I am going to walk my legs.

You're born into this world screaming and the fact is, nothing really changes! Babies, children, boy, girl, man or woman – we are all the same under the skin. What separates us is the varied ability to grow, learn and adapt to different situations and feelings. There is perhaps 20% mum, 20% dad, 60% a blank tape to be recorded. When things happen (they always do), that is when your true colours show. How you deal with your problem, the choices you've made and how you managed to calm that screaming baby is how you pick yourself back up again. These traits will show your true character, how strong you've become. There is only a set amount you can be taught, the rest is down to you.

Open your heart and try new things – you may get hurt, but if you don't you will never know. My one piece of advice is to take out some life insurance! After all, it's your life, you only get one. Do with it what you will – you never know, things might work out well in the end…

Bring forth onto me, everything, anything and all that you have. All that you are, I take all that you give. I may no longer be standing but through everything I still breathe. I still hold strong. My heart still beats and for each breath my lungs draw inside me, I live the life that I have pulled back from the brink of death. I came from the earth and to that I will return!

That cannot and will never change – in life we all have to die but I have come from the life I once lived with too much life still to live! They tried to take me five years ago…

I have lived, loved, been there and done that. I have experienced a few things in life and it has all lead me to this point. I have unfortunately lost friends and loved ones, but it has all happened and left me here. I am still going through everything that has passed. It has built the person I am today. I can't say whether that's good or bad, but either way my life continues as I am, upright or sitting. Those who were close are always going to be in my heart. Perhaps tomorrow I will hold onto the last thread of hope until that day my ashes join Philip in the wind and Tyler in the earth. Philip Henson was my best friend growing up but he tragically died in a car accident in 2001. From six years old there were a group of six of us friends. I am still in touch with Nick and Andrew.

I became the man I did because I shared Tyler's life, he motivated me and filled me with strength. Just the days I got up out of my bed for him – little things – but if you could live a day as I do, you realise the energy it takes just to motivate yourself! Sometimes the kindest thing to do for those you love is also the hardest – to let them go…

Blood flows through me as it does with every living thing, from the sap in a tree to water in a river, my blood is red and boils every day. I can't move but my mind is alive like a nest of bulldog ants eating a gecko from flesh to bone… My mind eats me alive…

Like the sands of time, running out one grain at a time.

CONTINUING ON

I need to make the life that I've been given back count; I can honour what Tyler did for me by carrying on. I need to do everything I can with what I've been given back – you never know when you will be taken! But when I go he'll be there, his suffering and pain gone. I held him while he took his last breath, whispering to him, "I love you… Go to sleep X." Without him or Tyler in my life now I would have de-railed and given it to what was coming long ago. One day I will be back with my puppy, Dexter… but for now, while I am soothed by the sound of Tyler's breathing, I need to continue with this life I have been given back, plus just to give me one last kick in the nuts as my catheter has blocked! The nurse is on her way to change it.

Please make your mark on this world, you only live once.

Stay strong as life is hard most of the time for everyone. We tend to remember the good times and forget the bad… My life before was far from perfect and now things are even less straightforward, but some things keep me pushing on. I think sometimes it's pure stubbornness – when people tell me I can't I want to even more, even with the bad stuff, drink, smoking, etc. People treat me differently now, telling me I can't drink or smoke but then I end up drinking more and burning myself, but I feel freer (not the next day – I'm hanging!) A day hung over makes me want to get back to it and make something of what I've been given back!

Cry when you need to, listen to your body and not other 'crazy talk' – I can talk shit as well; you just need to take all the positives you can from anything you can. Keep your family close – they need you as much as you need them. It's real difficult when your manhood is taken away and when people are talking down to you – it used to piss me off at first, but it's that attitude I use to drive me on. It can break you down to your true character. You'll see how much you can take…

In hospital I had a trachy (breathing tube in your neck instead of your mouth) and could only move my head. I had an air tube to blow into to get attention. Now I transfer myself, I get out on my own, I'm looking into driving, I can lift my own weight out of my chair, I can swim alone and I can sit unaided. All this came after broken C5/C6 vertebrae with a cyst blocking my spine, a titanium plate with screws and scar tissue! Things will improve! You always need to find something to hold onto. I have my old, snoring dog but I love him, plus the rest of my family, my mum, dad, two brothers and sister who are mentioned earlier.

WHAT'S POSSIBLE?

Let's consider the boundaries of what's possible. Physically, we think we know what can and can't be done. I have been faced with a problem that so many people think cannot be solved and for a lot of people that is true, but to this day I'm still pressing on those boundaries. Things change…

'Empty your cup' – Wing Tsun.

'Do not be tense, just be ready, not thinking but not dreaming, not being set but being flexible. It is being 'wholly' and quietly alive, aware and alert, ready for whatever may come' – Bruce Lee.

Age… time… everything passes you by! Do you know what I did this week? I actually watched the grass grow on the patch of dirt outside my window! (I also completed 17 miles on my FES bike).

THE SPOKEN WORD!

The strength in my words comes from the feelings inside me. I know I am who I am but not all that I will be. Walking, for me, would be a dream come true and that is my end goal! Each day now I work towards my independence.

Towards all that I can do, to be all that I can be, I bend and press on those medical boundaries every day – read this diary to see what can be achieved – I am going to get all that I can out of my body, to be strong in mind and heart. Every day it would be so much easier just to give up, to sit back and just let go. Not me! I'm not built that way.

> *'Be like a bumblebee; it flies but doesn't know it's seemingly physically impossible (tiny wings, big body)… but bumblebees don't care what we think.'*

With so much AD throughout each episode I was so happy when the pounding stopped and once the pressure inside my head stopped things felt so good. Having a spinal cord injury (SCI) is obviously something I'm never going to get away from. As my lovely matron at hospital once said, "You have to… you just get used to the pain." Such a lovely, caring woman! You may remember this was one of the sayings that seriously pissed me off earlier in this book, but, yes, it's so true.

Live through the pain and the heartache in life! It makes those quiet times in-between seem like heaven!

I'm Alexander Thomas Smith, and you're reading 'my life to date'.

Time waits for no-one.

I'm not giving up on medical science. They are advancing in all areas every day. In my physio sessions I am now maintaining what I have as each session brings me very similar results. On each Tuesday I am on the treadmill, then in-between I'm cycling away every day (most days) on my FES bike.

I need to have some solidarity, some routine to keep things in order. I am putting things in place to construct my exoskeleton, a wearable mobile machine that is powered by a system of electric motors, pneumatics, etc. It's a physio experiment that I couldn't previously use before because of lack of triceps and I couldn't stand with crutches. I have to get others to create what I can visualise; this, as you can imagine, doesn't go as quickly, or as efficiently as it should. So, while all those scientists are working away at my cure for paralysis, I'll maintain my health and fitness.

ODE TO MY LITTLE CYST

I'm here for you always. Closer to your head than your heart, wedged right there for you always… Burning into you like a fire in the darkest night, I'm there… When you're feeling lonely know that I'm there, cutting off your feeling, oh, and your motor function too! When people get to you… When the world is burning you down… I am the nerve pain… I am the fire – feel your burn, the hurt deep inside you; every day I am there, into you... Onto you… Nothing you can do… When you're alone in the dark… Lying, still unable to move… Know I am there, I am everything you hate… Everything you need… If I just left you, that's what you desire… If I let you go… The smallest spark lights the darkest night – fight with what you know… But I'm always going to be there… Right there for you, work around me, try and find a way… I'm always going to be there… Right there inside you – breaking you down, I am the burn… I am your pain! Love you, Alex. Your little cyst. Know where to find me C5/6.

'Bee all you can bee, even if you're a wasp!' – Alex Smith.

ME

Each day is mine! ‘Patience is a power all by itself’. I’m not the person I once was, but I AM the person that you now see; every day builds who I am.

It’s 02:25 hrs and I’m awake typing… I should be sleeping… The need to do more with the life I’ve been given back grows with the hours through the night – forget the now – bring on the future.

FIRE

I can't move my legs, but when I think about moving them, or any other paralysed part of me I can make it burn. It feels like an inferno all through my body. When I try to move my legs and feet (especially my right) it 'powers' up the energy in my spinal reflex and the muscle memory – or fairy dust! I'm usually able to move only once, sometimes more. Using this 'movement' I can turn myself in bed and it sometimes helps when transferring to another bed, and it hurts too. It's called nerve pain but pain is only reminding you that you're still alive. At times I do need that reminder… I WANT my legs and finger function; I'm not getting anywhere sitting around thinking, but sitting here typing my thoughts certainly helps. I NEED someone to love to share my life with but I cannot find someone until I learn to love myself first. Sitting here just typing can sometimes drive me mad. I NEED to have independence for my sanity, but in the meantime I have to accept who I am… but I don't! I know everyone has issues, everyone has problems and most can be resolved or be hidden away, but mine are in your face – they're all out there. I broke my neck and along with it went my heart!

I'm trapped in this 'open prison' called SCI. At present

there is no cure, but who knows? As I said, there are developments and research underway. Apparently people say "we're close" and "we're knocking on the door," but I have to keep my patience. I am classed as quadriplegic and I have pushed myself so far, holding onto the smallest thread of hope that one day I may be completely independent and that things may improve.

Tomorrow I will return to my bike and do another 18 miles, maintaining my blood circulation, bone density and muscle mass, keeping my legs in 'working order', just in case things improve with medical science.

I mentioned earlier that I don't feel I am an inspiration (to others) but I am my own inspiration and I have to keep going and remember that.

A positive fact I hold onto – three years ago I could only move my head and now I am pushing myself to walk. I will have my independence.

Of course, most days I do regret going swimming that day, but I wouldn't be the person I am today if I hadn't...

PHYSIO SESSIONS

I've just finished yet another physio session. It consisted of assisted standing and walking. Today I left off my leg braces (trial and error) to see how things would go, but I found out that (for now) I still need them; they help to align my body on the treadmill, keeping my legs in more of a uniform walking pattern. Also they help channel my weight down through my legs, which takes my weight off the harness allowing my legs to work and letting my groin breathe and blood flowing. Without the braces I walk bow-legged (like a cowboy – squashing my bits, making me into a cowgirl!) Also I have a few blood pressure problems so next Tuesday I'll be trying again with the braces on!

I also stand using parallel bars with leg braces and the standing chair to test my autonomic system. I can now work on the mats. I'm doing a lot on the floor anyway!

RECOVERY AND IMPROVEMENT

There has been NEW RECOVERY after (nearly) three years! As I already mentioned, since the accident, all down my left side I've always had more sensation and this has steadily improved over the past three years to approximately 77% sensation throughout my body. My right leg, however, has had less sensation but more muscle tone (and more control in the quads).

This morning I'm getting a lot of nerve pain and down my right side (torso) my stomach muscles ARE BACK IN MY CONTROL! I have been told that after 18 months/two years, things stop 'recovering' but, as I said – THREE YEARS! And I have new motor function back, so, as I've said all the way through, alexwillwalkAGAIN and BOLLOCKS TO NEGATIVE PEOPLE! I am Alex and alexwillwalkagain and I will walk again.

I used to smoke a good 20–40 cigarettes per day (another result of my accident – my diaphragm is paralysed, I've had trouble breathing. While in hospital my whole respiratory system gave up). Now I'm free from tobacco. Just a deep breath now feels so good and some great things in life are free too (sexy time is free… until the pitter-patter of those tiny feet).

Life is fragile, life is short, life is harsh, life won't make sense, life needs pain and when things happen in life you have to accept what hand you're dealt. You need to adapt to the twists and turns and stand up and face your problems – they won't go away otherwise unless you deal with them. One thing though… once you've dealt with your problem from today, tomorrow will only bring more.

I don't live my life through Facebook any more; I want to live the life I had, the life that I was building, the plans that I was making.

NIGHT-TIME THOUGHTS

It's 03:03 hrs… Sometimes the harder you try to sleep the harder it gets! People think, worry and fear things… anything from being late in the morning for work or about the way they look, to the big spider that could be there in the dark. Maybe someone outside is trying to take what's not theirs, down to the old wiring setting the place on fire.

I'm typing this now but while I was lying down there were so many things going through my head. The main one (apart from the fact I couldn't get to sleep!) is how on fire I feel because of the nerve pain and that my drugs are wearing off (from the 22:00 hrs dose). I felt twisted in bed too. I've dealt with this since January 2006. When I woke from my coma my consultant told me, "You will never even roll in bed." Can you believe that someone would say that? Just one of the many knock-backs I've received.

I do still feel slightly twisted but that's probably got something to do with the 27kg 'baby Tyler' in my bed (he's sleeping so I won't wake him), but I do sleep on my side (my 'good' side… they are both 'good'!?… my left side). I have not only got up to type this but the baby is still sleeping! BOLLOCKS again to those who think I won't walk – I will walk!

Every little goal needs to be seen along the way. It all helps to drive me forward – it takes sooooo long though – the strength I feel today is what I will use tomorrow to drive forward, faster, further each day.

I'm not worrying about, what for me are trivial things – the spiders, the burglars or being late anywhere… I can't stand not being able to do the things I want, need or like. I can't breathe some nights because my nasal cavities block up and my lungs aren't strong enough (yet) to clear them. Another frustration is that sometimes I can't even pick the simplest thing up.

My dad is in the process of building a house/gym for my independence and rehab. This is never where I saw myself. At the point of my accident I was looking into buying a 4-bedroom cave house in Spain!

I've had money, I've lost money (a lot of times had no money) and I was earning money (things were looking good…) then took a turn for the worse. Life can be really shit but it just makes the good times feel better and the good thing about the human mind is it tends to (mainly) remember the good times.

Take strength from meeting the challenges and move ahead. The struggles you face are just what you need to fulfil your potential for greatness. A year from now, when you look back at today, you'll see that the problem you're concerned with right now was another valuable lesson waiting to be learned.

Sometimes the best times are when you're asleep, but your dreams, good or bad, will find you there. Dream of walking… dream of flying… but to dream of escaping is all that you can do… to dream of your dream – everyone has one – it will bring you home. It will not fix your problems but will comfort your worries and push you forward, to continue on the path you have chosen and to keep going each day… waiting, waiting and waiting for things to happen. Dream of tomorrow but live for today. Things will happen but perhaps not the way you want them to.

Let me tell you of one other thing I did in my younger years. The day before my birthday on June 24th in the middle of a storm, the rain felt like nails all over me; the wind was so strong that the corn fields were flat… and Andrew Butcher and I found ourselves running through a field with trees falling behind us and lightning striking the ground around us – we ran as fast as our little legs would carry us!

Now I get pushed from room to room… I will be back! Stand up or lay down and take it – your choice.

Often, I feel like shouting, "I am not paralysed! I am ALEXANDER THOMAS SMITH! On December 14th 2006 my life changed… it did not finish."

PAST TWELVE MONTHS

For the past twelve months from January 2019, I have been hospitalised with pneumonia, then discharged with a grade three pressure sore, only to be bedridden again for three months to heal. Throughout this time I dropped all my medication down to just the present day 5mg oxybutynin. My advice is to always consult your doctor before adjusting medication because there could be repercussions – they are the experts! I also changed my diet and dropped 24kg! In May I started counselling, posttraumatic stress disorder (PTSD), trauma and hypnosis therapy. I decided to shake everything up as I couldn't go on living the same days over and over. I have also taken a driving assessment to regain some type of independence…

Don't lose sight of what is right in front of you. I have been on the very edge of despair; I even once took a step over that line into the darkest part of life, which I only briefly mentioned previously... I found my way back, only by the guidance from the most beautiful thing in life – 'a chance for life itself' – in the darkness. A hand came through and pulled me out and into the light – the hand of Urška. Yes, that's right. The best part of this year was meeting the girl who walked into my life and stole my heart! Urška Omerzi – once a carer, now a very important part of my life. She sees me for who I am inside, beyond the boundaries of paralysis and showing me that a life is still there, to not only live, but one still to be built on and be proud of! Urška has shown me that, as bad as life can be, it can still pull you through. It is merely the beginning of the next chapter in your life. As this handbook on my paralysis draws to a close, the next chapter opens as a future untold just beginning…

Urška and me

MY VIEW OF THE COMA

INSIDE THE COMA – THE DREAM WORLD

Nobody knows what happens when you die, but for me, at least through the fight for my life in Miami, my heart stopped no less than six times, using adrenaline injections to the heart and everything and anything else they did got me back again. I do have 'weird' memories – morphine dreams...

I'd be anywhere in my dream world; each time they zapped my heart my dream froze… All I saw was a bright green or blue TV screen/light, then I found myself re-starting things (in my dream) again from a secret Special Forces cinema in South America. There were doctors, surgeons and family around me at the time. It felt that Tyler had gone, as with anyone close… but I too will go. My energy needs to go somewhere…

Reflecting back on my coma, I remember the vivid dreams I had. On reflection, these dreams related to what was happening by my bedside. A selection of these are found below.

There are more dreams to come, but the reason for this section is to inform you that talking to your loved ones while they are (at least) medically induced into a coma, that they can still hear you – it may not help too much but they can hear you.

In my dreams I was always rich; had two planes, three yachts (big ones) and a train.

Just before I start, you have to understand I was on a large cocktail of drugs...

During a blood transfusion, my sister, Jennifer, was standing next to my bed. People would talk to me all the time throughout my time in the coma. As my blood was leaving my body and the new blood came in, Jennifer was describing every gory detail, but in my dreams I was laying on a table next to her... and I was watching her blood coming into my body.

I once dreamt I was in Alaska. Each night I would go to bed and sleep but by about 04:00–05:00 hrs an old Indian man called X-ray would appear and get out of my bed. He would shut my head in a foam vice and go off ice fishing! He would never allow me to go with him (I just thought the foam vice was to protect me in case of an avalanche). As you can see from reading the story through my sister's eyes (My sister's diary), I used to get X-rayed nearly every day and the guy would come in around 04:00–05:00 and shout "X-ray!" at me. The bed I was in secured my head with a foam vice.

My mum would reassure me all the time by telling me that I had an accident in Sint Maarten but was now in Miami and that I'd be home soon. This would really confuse me. While I was dreaming I would be anywhere from India to South America, then all of a sudden I was back in Miami?!

I also dreamt that I had got married to a very attractive young lady (Sarah Riley) and we had two beautiful daughters. I owned a Caribbean island (you see, I told you I was always rich in my dreams) and for some reason we left one daughter there. Unfortunately we split up, as I was too busy fighting a war down in South America. I don't remember dreaming about Sarah before my accident but while I was in Miami she used to visit every Sunday. On one such visit she left as I flatlined (possibly when we split in the dream).

This bizarre dream began about me coming home from sea. My brother and I got into some trouble and ended up fighting with these other guys. I stepped in and tried to calm things down (this was in a field and I was standing on a transit van). As everything was calming someone shot me in the chest with a shotgun. As I was in a critical condition, a tent was erected and they operated then and there. A Canadian surgeon and a Chinese lady headed up the medical team. They 'saved' me but made me into a type of seal-like pig man! Because of my new appearance I apparently didn't care much for myself. This lead to me living under my parents' house in a basement-type flat with a big pool (for the seal part of me). I started filming the things I was doing and this lead to a series of jackass-type films. These films made me a lot of money hence the yachts, a train and two planes (a red one and a blue one), two Caribbean islands, plus enough money to have more surgery to change back to normal. Well, I said it was bizarre…

Another dream I remember is when I joined the American Special Forces and got based down in South America. On leave I would go back to one of my yachts. In my will I had left my planes to my brothers. During my dreams I died three times during which everything froze – all I could see were bright green or blue screens, then I woke up in a cinema!

When in South America if I was in trouble, I'd call for that big, orange guy from Fantastic Four, or my brothers in the planes (by now the planes were theirs). Another time, on leave, I ended up on my yacht in the Everglades in Florida where I crashed the yacht and had my foot eaten by a crocodile! In my dream, where there are no logical outcomes, I was too busy to sort out my foot and so went around with a skeleton foot.

Each time I 'died' I would be transported back to their base in a large noisy cinema, all the time being followed by a Canadian guy and a Filipino woman who were always trying to kill me!

Like the X-ray dream, another connection with my real life was that the TV (my cinema) was on in my room and my surgeon was Dr L (a Canadian) and the doctor from my ship that flew with me to Miami was from the Philippines!

The peculiar dreams don't end there! Another dream to mention and one that ties in with a previous one, is that I was on a yacht (three of which belonged to my aunt and uncle from New York, Anne and Pat Dockery. While on the yacht I was sailing through the Florida Everglades. I was in the engine room and the boat crashed resulting with a large hole in the bottom. I was stuck as the hull started to fill with water and an alligator swam in and ate my foot! Just the flesh though... Again, I was too busy to get it fixed. Instead I walked around from then on with a skeleton foot in my boots.

Down in South America the Filipino lady (who I later found out lived in my roof) injected me with formaldehyde causing a death-like look. Thinking I was dead they threw me out into the jungle for meat, thinking the jungle animals would eat the meat. The community was actually a local tribe of cannibals! When one guy found my body and realised I was still alive (just), he brought me back to the door of this bunker/cinema and explained that I was still living. The Canadian guy was at the door and wouldn't let me back in. I believe, in real life, when they used the defibrillator and adrenaline it pulled me out of my coma for a brief moment, the TV being overheard each time.

Back to the dream, I was paralysed from the formaldehyde at this point, the tribesman (a cannibal) couldn't bring himself to snap my neck and take me so he held me and stayed there, trying to bring himself to do it for what seemed like the whole day. Anywhere in the world my dreams would take me, I always heard "You've had an accident, we are in Miami, we'll be home soon," then back in the cinema I went. It was my mum who had said this to me throughout. (By the way, my mum had also written a diary throughout but it was on a whole emotional level, bless her, and one dribbled with tears throughout).

Tizer (the red fizzy drink) was injected into my bloodstream one time, the idea being it would stop my heart with the bubbles. Three little girls saw this and spoke out while in hospital. After this the girls came with me everywhere I went, carrying defibrillators for each time I 'died'!

The drug-induced coma brought on dreams that felt like memories.

This was the base for the rest of my dreams… I do have to repeat they were extremely drug-fuelled dreams. If you also read My sister's diary later on you will see how closely the morphine dreams relate.

EPILOGUE

As I mentioned earlier, at the time of writing, the current global pandemic that is COVID-19 has hit and isolation and quarantine came to everyone throughout the globe (four weeks' isolation due to the pandemic, another three weeks just added – 13 years and possibly 40 more for me).

This new virus will be extremely dangerous, and especially after lockdown with carers in and out, I hope that no one will bring it to me... I will require more mental strength at the fear of the unknown. For now though, what will be will be. With a normally functioning person it can be difficult, and a person over 70 with underlying health issues could suffer, but living with high care needs and paralysis in my lung diaphragm (C5/6) is a whole other level of worry.

If you're in a similar position, just try living each day as it comes, plan for a future but live in the now. Adapt and change as you need to and try and see what lies ahead for you.

When I sum up my care throughout my recovery, I see how far I've come, from the beginnings of only being able to move my head when returning home, to a 24 hr live-in carer – one for two hours in the morning (08:00–10:00), one at night (20:00–22:00) and two nurses in the early morning (02:00–

04:00) to turn me in bed. Government physio guidelines on returning home were that only six sessions were to happen once weekly! My family were paying for a neurophysio twice weekly for eight years to bring recovery and independence throughout.

If you would like to follow me, I have a YouTube channel with videos of my daily movements and handling called TheAlextsmith25 (cap sensitive). This shows the substantial change in my life now compared to the first few months after the accident.

My present day living is with just one 24-hr carer as independently and physically possible, fighting for true independence one day.

Remember:

Be who you are, for only you can be you.

Life happens... it just does. The best things happen when you aren't even looking.

MY SISTER'S DIARY

(written by Jennifer-Kate Smith)

Please note these extracts are lifted exactly as they appear in her diary.

Monday December 18th 2006

This is four days after the accident but we only just got the notebook; breathing was very tough for you today and you were still very agitated with the breathing tube – understandably, great strength in your arms. They have put restraints on your arms to stop you pulling out your breathing tube but we take them off when we come in and hold your hand. Your right arm was so strong I couldn't hold it away from you trying to pull out your ventilator so Dad had to hold it down instead!

Blood pressure 130/83

Tuesday December 19th 2006 – Nurses Felicia and Michelle

They took a sample of your lungs today and did X-rays, also a CT scan and found you have ARDS (acute respiratory distress syndrome). Chest CT showed it was more like pus than fluid in your lungs, so they can't just suction it out with a chest drain, they have to suction it out at your breathing tube. The ventilator is doing all the breathing for you and that means your body can rest. They have found signs of infection so have started you on antibiotics. Michelle ordered an X-ray on your left hand because it's so swollen; it may just be fluid from where you are not moving around but she just wanted to check. The infection could be pneumonia but it will be a few days before the sample from the lungs can tell us.

Blood pressure 135/70

Wednesday December 20th 2006

You had a comfortable night last night, there is more colour in your face too which is nice. The swelling in your hands and tummy have reduced slightly today as well. We saw Dr L today, he was the one who operated on your spine. He said it would be a few days before the antibiotics kicked in. They decreased your oxygen input to 60% this afternoon – so far so good. Elliot and Ross arrived today, they were shocked to see you but glad they were able to be there with you. Calm and resting when we left.

Temp 37.2°

Wednesday December 21st 2006 – Nurse Janice

A lady came today to see Dad and I. She's from the spinal rehabilitation unit. She said when the time is right she will be with you for rehabilitation and in terms of surgery it's all done and they are pleased with how it went. The main focus right now is your lungs and medical condition, the spine can wait for now. She briefly said about rehab and that the neck collar would have to stay on for three months. You are so strong and determined and today trying to breathe over the ventilator instead of letting the machine help you to rest. Mum and Dad were outside the room talking to Steve Price from Holland America Lines' risk assessment team. I was alone in the room with you and your breathing tube popped off! I was very scared but the doctors and nurses are brilliant and fixed it in no time. It happened because of your moving in bed and weight on one side making it pop off, but they have attached it to the bed now so it moves with you. They increased your oxygen input also until you are a bit calmer as you were again trying to breathe over the machine and we need the oxygen you're getting to go straight to your lungs – when you fight it the oxygen goes around your body instead of to your lungs. You are now on two antibiotics; one for a urine infection and the other a general one for your whole body until they are sure where and what it needs. Sharonne Hanson and her husband Max flew in today from Seattle; she is the crew medical officer from Holland America Line. The colour in your cheeks is better again today and you are passing more fluid, which shows the urine infection is clearing and the antibiotics are starting to work. Tonight was a bit scary; they put you on full life support and into a coma. You probably won't remember but up until now you were awake, unable to talk because of the breathing tube but aware of what's going on. They put you into the coma and on life support to help you as you are so determined to breathe over the ventilator and for yourself. Unfortunately this is not helping you so now you will heal faster and allow your body to heal and rest.

Blood pressure 130140/120ish
Temp 37.9°

Friday December 22nd 2006 – Nurses Albert and Lesley

You have two nurses today as this is a training hospital and Lesley is training Albert; they are fully qualified nurses, it's just they need special training for the intensive care unit. Both Albert and Lesley are really good and answer all our questions and always giving Mum hugs. You are on full life support now and in the coma. All your numbers as in blood pressure, temp, oxygen levels have been stable all day. They got the results back from the sample of your lungs and it was good; it had no clear signs of infection and the X-ray showed no predominant signs of pneumonia, so it looks like your lungs are just poorly from the water you swallowed at the time of the accident. They call it secondary drowning but the respiratory therapist said it didn't sound like there was much water in your lungs – the shock to the lungs and water combined caused the condition ARDS. So they are carrying on with your antibiotics and we spoke to Dr L and he said, depending on how you do over the next few days, will decide on whether they put a trachy in which reduces the risk of infection and makes you more comfortable. They did an X-ray of your tummy and everything is fine. They sent off more samples (they call them cultures here in the USA) of your blood and lungs (BAL) just to check again for any signs of infection. They have ordered another chest X-ray for the morning to see if there is any improvement in your lungs yet; they do at least one early morning every day. Your blood oxygen levels (sats) have been good today so they are going to lower your oxygen input a little bit to see how you do. They will do hourly blood tests. This evening your blood levels (or blood gas) have been good so they have decided to lower your 'peep levels' (that is the amount of pressure the ventilator uses for each breath) so, by reducing pressure it allows your lungs to have a go at giving a bit of breath on their own. They have so far reduced from 18 to 16 and you are doing really well so later tonight they will take it back to 15. Your temperature has gone up a little this evening so they are going to get you a cooling blanket.

Nurse tonight – Laura
Blood pressure 135/80

Saturday December 23rd 2006 – Nurses Lesley and Albert

You had a setback tonight at 10:10 (22:10 hrs), your pulse dropped to 21 and your heart stopped. They got you back very quickly though and you've been stable throughout the night. They put a mask over your face, gave you pure oxygen and gave you an injection that goes into your chest and that's how they get your heart going again. They have put a new machine in your room, an external pacemaker. This monitors your pulse rate and when it drops below 50 it will kick in and give you a boost that keeps your heart going. I think it's because of being in the coma that this happened – the rest of your body isn't doing anything so your heart thought it would have a rest too! Dr L did say that patients who injure their spine usually have low blood pressure and pulse rate, they warned us it could happen again though. They are prepared with the pacemaker and have an injection by your bedside to give you if it does. Your peep levels are the same as yesterday, 16, and you are doing fine so they are happy. It's 18:00 hrs now and your oxygen levels are at 80% on the ventilator. The plan is to reduce it to 65% slowly to see how you do, and taking hourly blood tests before they change it.

Sats 97%–100%
Blood pressure 133/73

Sunday December 24th 2006 – Nurse Max

The respiratory nurse came and said there is a tiny improvement in your lungs today and your nose isn't runny so no infection in your sinuses. Sarah Riley came from the ship today, just as we were leaving at the end of visiting (09:30–10:00). Your pulse dropped again and your heart stopped but they were fantastic – got the crash cart, cleared everyone from the floor and were 100% on you and stabilised you in no time (although it felt forever). I just thought maybe I shouldn't have said that but this is a book for you and I want to be as honest about everything that happened. Your oxygen levels in your blood have been good so far today. Dr L said they would do the trachy on Wednesday depending on what emergencies come in. It's going to be a long road to recovery but I know in my heart you'll get through this and make it. This started as a notebook to remember questions to ask the doctors but now it will be a diary from me to you so you can see how far you have come. I love you and will be here with you every step of the way.

Blood pressure 147/88

Monday December 25th 2006 – Nurse Max

You had a stable night last night and all your numbers were stable throughout the day. Your oxygen input is 75% and sats 95% or above all day so far. You are still on full life support and in the coma but all the time like this your body has vital healing time to get better. I'm not sure how long they will keep you like this, I guess when they feel your lungs are strong enough for you to be awake. It may be days or even weeks, it's just a waiting game at the minute. You take as long as you need; I and we are not going anywhere so however long it takes is how long it will be.

Blood pressure 147/93

Temp 37.4°

Tuesday December 26th 2006 – Nurses Elizabeth and Stephanie

You had a stable night last night and your temperature is back down to 37°. It sneezed up to 37.8° when they took the cooling blanket off. Dr L said they would do the trachy either Thursday or Friday depending on what other emergencies come in. Your white blood cell count is 26000 and it should be 11000, so shows signs of infection somewhere. You are still passing all the fluid they are giving you well, the stuff that is coming up when they suction your lungs is a lot lighter in colour and not as much of it, so shows the antibiotics are working in your lungs. The blood gas tests have been good and your oxygen levels (sats) have been between 98%–99% – I even saw 100% a couple of times! Your oxygen input is down to 75% and the doctors are pleased. The nurse tested your blood sugar level and it was a little high so they had to give you some insulin; it was 204. Apparently the medication you are on causes it to go up and the fact you aren't eating any normal food or moving to get rid of the excess sugar causes your blood sugar to be high, but it's common in patients like you and won't be a permanent thing. Your eyes and right hand seem quite puffy but apparently the paralytics (coma medication) cause that.

Wednesday December 27th 2006 – Nurse Max

Your pulse dropped to 30 at 02:00 hrs this morning but you did not crash which is a good thing and they stabilised you quickly and you have been stable ever since. They have changed the way your ventilator is helping you breathe this morning; before you were getting a high pressurised breath 18 times a minute but they have changed that to 30 times a minute at a lower pressure. This is more like what the lungs would do naturally themselves. They did a chest X-ray this morning and found you had a PNEUMOTHORAX which is air in the lung; this could probably be the reason your pulse and oxygen levels go so low and even for you crashing, so they have put you in a chest drain, which is a tube that goes in your chest and drains out any excess fluid and helps move the air from the outside of your lungs (pneumothorax). It also decreases the chances of your pulse dropping again and of your lung collapsing which it had done slightly. You woke up at around 11:30am today (for a little while unexpectedly) because you are so strong. You built up a tolerance to the medication they are giving you to keep you in the coma. Your nurse Max who is brilliant said he explained to you where you were and what had happened and he said you were very calm the whole time then went back off to sleep again.

Thursday December 28th 2006 – Nurse Janice

You had the trachy fitted today, so you will be so much more comfortable without that tube in your mouth – Dr L did it. We met Dr G, he is the medical director of neurointensive care where you are – he said you are doing GREAT! He's really pleased with how you are doing and the new way the ventilator is going and said maybe in a few days, if your oxygen levels stay above 94% for at least 24 hrs, then they might consider taking you out of the coma. Because you have been in the coma for a week now you have built up a tolerance to the drugs and have woken up a bit. When we talk to you you move your eyebrows and twitch your nose. The doctors say as long as you stay calm and your numbers stay steady that they are happy not to increase your sedation any more.

Oxygen 98%–100%

Pulse 65–80, temp 36.4°

Blood pressure 133/83

Friday December 29th 2006 – Nurses Lee and Elizabeth

Your blood pressure and your pulse dropped again today at 05:00 hrs but they managed to stabilise you before you crashed. They have put your oxygen input back up to 100% and your sats levels are at 100%. The nurse has just sent off the blood gas test, if all good then they will reduce the oxygen input again from your ventilator slowly. Dr G (medical director of intensive care), Dr L and Dr Z are having a chat about what the next step should be. They might do another ultrasound of your legs (they did one a couple of days ago just to check for clots; they thought chances were unlikely but wanted to check everything) just to make sure there was nothing else that could be causing your pulse to drop. They also mentioned doing a CT of your upper body to check for clots, but could just be happening due to the salt water that you swallowed and that got into your lungs. It could be pneumonia and ARDS, just the ARDS or pulmonary embolus (clot in lungs), so checking everything. They stopped your dopamine for a while today (this is medication to help your blood pressure stay above 100/? and you did well when you were off of it. They put it back on but with a much lower dose. It's too early for you to be off it yet but they like to push and see what you can do on your own, which makes sense. They gave you a bit more sedation this evening to make you more comfortable as you were a bit frustrated.

Oxygen 100%
Pulse 72
Blood pressure 129/62
Temperature 36.3°

Saturday December 30th 2006 – Nurses Lee and Elizabeth

You had a good stable night last night and your numbers are all steady today. They have given you a blood transfer today – apparently your red blood cell count is 7.6 and normal is around 12, but I'm only surprised it took this long – they do so many blood tests each day so I'm not surprised you need a top up! The white blood cell count is down to 13000 today and it should be around 11000 so that is really good. White blood cell count shows if there is infection anywhere and it was, like, 28000 a few days ago so you are doing well and the antibiotics are obviously doing their job. The respiratory therapist came and changed your breathing tube. When she suctioned you she said not a lot came out compared to a few days ago. Your lungs also sound better than they have in a while, she said she could HEAR oxygen moving around in there! Elizabeth is the trainee nurse today, like Albert the other day. They have to do eight months' training for ICU and only get one chance at it, if they fail any of their exams along the way they are out. Elizabeth is thorough and very dedicated and we really like her. Lee, who is training her is really nice too and a really good teacher. She told Mum today that you could be in intensive care for anywhere from 3–8 months which was a bit of a shock. We knew it was going to take time but we didn't realise it could be that much. That doesn't really matter though, however long it takes we'll be here for you every step of the way.

Oxygen 100%
Pulse 55–60
Temperature 36.9°
Blood pressure 120/70

P.S. The doctor came around today and said the X-ray from this morning did show a slight improvement from previous ones! (They do them most days).

Sunday December 31st 2006 – Nurse Lee

You had a good stable night last night and the nurse said your lungs are sounding clearer. Sarah Riley and Captain Henk came today. Sarah brought English cigarettes, brandy and face cream for Mum, which was really nice of her. Then this afternoon Mike Abraham, Martin, Michael and Willem (Chief Engineer and his wife) came, they brought another copy of the photo Sarah made for you. At the moment you are still stable – that is what we want as it will be a while yet before your lungs are back to full health, so as long as you're stable you are not getting any worse. They just reduced the oxygen input from the ventilator from 75% down to 70% and so far you are tolerating it really well. Your sats has been 100%. They seem to be reducing your oxygen much more slowly now which makes more sense, this gives you more time to get used to it. Your temperature is a little low this afternoon at 35.8°, but I'm not surprised, the air-con is so cold so the nurse Lee is getting you a couple of blankets to warm you up. Lee (nurse) also gave you a shave this morning, it was the first one since you arrived and you were growing a bit of a ginger beard!

Oxygen 100%
Blood pressure 120/75
Pulse 70
Blood sugar 120
White blood cell count 11400

Monday January 1st 2007 – Nurse Charmaine

You had a good stable night last night, I rang before and after midnight to make sure. Mum and I stayed up until after 12:00 and watched the ball drop on New York's Times Square (the ball is lifted up and dropped on the countdown to midnight) and there were loads of fireworks outside. You have come off your dopamine, which is the medication that keeps your blood pressure and pulse rate up, you are holding your blood pressure up at around 130/80, which is great, and your pulse is strong at 75–80. Your white blood cell count is down again today to 10400, which is great and means the infection is clearing. They have reduced your IV fluids as well as you are passing much more liquids, so that's another sign of infection clearing. The pacemaker has also been disconnected today, still in place though, just in case you need it, so there have been a few positive things today. I just hope and pray that the New Year carries on like this for you. They increased your sedation to make you more comfortable. Keep strong Alex, we love you very much and will be here for however long you need to get better.

Oxygen input 60%
Blood oxygen (sats) 100%
Blood sugar 104
Blood pressure 130/80
Pulse 75–80

Tuesday January 2nd 2007 – Nurse Charmaine

A good stable day today, your oxygen is down to 55% (input from ventilator) for the first time and you are tolerating it well, which is great! The nurse said the doctors are thinking about clamping your chest drain. If they do, they clamp it for a few hours then take an X-ray and if the lungs look good they will remove it, so that's a step forward.

I had to go to the dentist today as I had an abscess on my wisdom tooth. She said the tooth has to come out so we need to go to another dentist in a place called Coral Gables for that, but she gave me antibiotics for the meantime. Your temperature sneezed up a little this afternoon, the doctor said that when you injure your spine it's common for your temperature to go up and down easily. All your other numbers have been steady all day.

Pulse 65–70
White blood cell count 10400
Blood pressure 130/75
Oxygen (sats) 100%

Wednesday January 3rd 2007 – Nurse Monica

Your pulse rate dropped this morning to 20 but the nurse bagged you (put the oxygen pump on) quickly and it came straight back up and you've been stable ever since. Your oxygen input is now down to 45% which is incredible, that's the lowest it's been since you've been here and your blood oxygen is at 96%–98%, so you are doing really well. Dr G came in today and decided to change your ventilator back to how it was when you arrived (the respiratory therapist said it was complicated but basically back to how it started, so it's now the high pressure breaths and less of them). You do some of the breaths with the machine as well, the nurse today said she was amazed at how well you respond (move your eyebrows, nose, mouth and sometimes even nod), even though you are supposed to be in the coma and most people would be out cold on half the amount of medication. That just shows how strong and determined you really are. Dr O said your lungs are showing definite signs of improvement.

Thursday January 4th 2007 – Nurse Margaret

I had to go and have my wisdom tooth out today. He was a really nice dentist and it was all over and done in no time but I was very sleepy as he knocked me out with IV drip sedation. Mum said she wishes he was her dentist. You had a good stable day. Dad said he and Ross had palpitations at one stage because all your machines went crazy, but it was a technical fault that was fixed by a technician and not a medical problem that needed a doctor, so that's good. They tried to reduce the coma drugs today and change them for a heavy sedation; somewhere between all that Dad and Ross both saw you curl your toes and move your left foot, they said they both thought they were seeing things and both looked at each other and said "Did you see that? I saw that, did you?!" Who knows what that means but all we can do is hope and pray it will be a sign of things to come.

Elliot went out for a beer with Ross and Dad disappeared off with some locals. Ross woke up at 05:00 hrs and he still wasn't back so went and had a look around and couldn't find him, then came back to the apartment and five minutes later he walked in – he'd gone to some clubs after the pub! So he spent most of the day in bed and went in for a night visit. He said your night nurse was a really nice guy who told him "You were like a wild lion who had been sedated but would soon be alive and free again." It was awful for me not to see you today, it broke my heart, but I had to be sedated for my tooth so I was like a zombie all day and would have been useless there. But you know I was there with you even though I wasn't there, don't you?

Friday January 5th 2007 – Nurse Daisy

You had a quiet stable night last night. Dad, Elliot and Ross flew home today, it was hard to say goodbye but we will see them soon I hope!

Lucia rang this morning to say she was coming on the 14th for two weeks. Mum burst into tears when she spoke to her, she is very emotional essentially with Dad and the boys going today. You had a stable day. They had planned to move your feeding tube from your mouth to your tummy today but couldn't because you are still connected to the pacemaker. Your blood gas was normal which is fantastic and your blood oxygen input is 45%, which is brilliant. Your temperature, blood pressure and pulse were all good and stable all day too.

Saturday January 6th 2007 – Nurse Stephanie

You had an uneventful night last night, which is always good to hear. Your oxygen input is back up to 50% today as your sats went down to 90%, but that is still really good. Your pulse has been steady all day, between 65–80. Your blood pressure went a little low earlier but nothing drastic and it came back up on its own. Auntie Grace up in New York said she may come down next weekend and Jacinta said she would come after Dad has been back again (I think he is aiming for the first week in February), so you will have lots of visitors. I just wonder, hope and pray that you will be awake to see them.

White blood cell count 800
Temperature 36.2°
Blood pressure 123/77
They did an X-ray as we left, of your lungs.

Sunday January 7th 2007 – Nurses Stephanie Cavine

You had another uneventful night, your nurse was Cavine. Dr S came in and he said he wasn't going to change any of your settings and give you a nice well deserved rest, and he also said the reason your sats went a bit low yesterday was because of your chest drain tube; A – it was leaking slightly so they put a few more stitches around it; B – the suction setting on it was not on. Sarah, Florin, Danny and Martin came from the ship this afternoon. It's my birthday today, I've had better but

I'm going to have two birthdays this year, maybe a summer one for a change. Mum went to Walgreens, the shop down the road and bought me some silly things like bubble gum teeth, a candle and two toothbrushes and I got cards from Dad and the boys before they left. But all I really want for my birthday is for you to be better, but I know that won't happen suddenly overnight (however much I want it to, which is more than anything in this world and I hope and pray that it does). So I guess you having a stable night is great for now. The chest X-ray they did last night and this morning were both ok. Your white blood cell count was a little higher today but your red blood cell count was good, so the transfusion they gave you obviously did its job like I told you it would, and make you stronger.

Temperature 36.6°
Oxygen input 50%
Sats 95%–98%
Blood pressure 145/82–112/67

Monday January 8th 2007 – Nurse Stephanie

I have started a fresh new page today as something happened today which, please God, is a fresh new start for you – you woke from the coma! When I rang up this morning as I do every morning when I wake up and every night before I go to sleep, Stephanie said you had a good stable night but were a bit agitated but she didn't know why. From that moment on we were wanting to get there and of course when we wanted to get there, typically the car was late. When we walked in I saw your arms moving and I remember Stephanie saying they have reduced your sedation and woken you up, but I was just standing by your bed. I just couldn't believe your eyes were finally open, you kept trying to talk but no one could understand you so I came closer and you looked me in the eyes and said "GET THIS FUCKING TUBE OUT MY MOUTH!" I repeated what you said and just saw the relief in your face that finally someone understood you. You can't talk because you have the trachy in and are still on the ventilator, but you can mouth what you want to say. I have a feeling I'm going to become your personal lip-reader and I will be your voice for you until you are able to talk again, which I'm sure won't be too long; you have already surpassed all the doctors' expectations of you. Only a few days ago they said it would be weeks before they even considered waking you from your coma, but I guess my birthday wish came true (a couple of hours late, but I'll let you off – better late then never). Whenever anyone asked what I wanted or was getting for my birthday, I said "Nothing, all I want is a conversation with my brother," and today that happened. I know there is still a very high ladder to climb but this is definitely a step up! So anyway, as soon as Stephanie heard what you said she suggested taking that one out of your mouth and putting a smaller one in your nose and you said "Yes." Within half an hour they had it swapped over. They had to wait a while and then do an X-ray to check if it was in the right place before they started your food going in again, so you're now back on your 'Baileys' diet again. A little while later you asked me "Am I going to die?" I told you straight away "NO!" You are getting stronger every day, we are not going anywhere until the day we take you home with us. Mum asked what you said and I just looked at her as if to say 'I'll tell you later'. Bless her, she can't see what you say, especially with her glasses on! Only Mum would have to take her glasses OFF to see! We explained to you that you had an accident in St Maarten and were now in Miami but that you still have a lot of medication in your system and “I think it will be a few days until it’s out of your system,” and you actually start taking in what has happened. I had to scratch your eyes, nose and head and I’ve never been so happy to scratch someone else’s itch in my life.

This evening you told me “I need to go to the toilet.” I asked if it was a wee and you told me “Yes,” so Mum explained all about the catheter and that whenever you needed to go you could and it would go straight into the bag, and it just so happened, Stephanie had just emptied the bag. The relief spread across your face as the bag filled up and you weed! We were so excited, you knew you needed a wee and were holding it until you knew it was ok to go and then you went! FANTASTIC! Stephanie and the other nurses didn’t seem very excited like us though; apparently it could just be a phantom thing (not in my opinion given the relief on your face and watching that bag fill up) or could be a positive sign, they just say it’s too early to tell yet. Three occupational therapists and one physio came in to assess you in the afternoon. They did not realise you had only just woken from the coma and said they would be back in a few days. Very pretty girls, I think you will appreciate them a bit more when you’re more awake. Today was a real mixture of emotions because it is fantastic to see your eyes open and to be able to communicate with you but at the same time it was so hard to see you so agitated and us not able to help you. I promise we will do everything we can for you and I will not go back home without you. I’m here for you 200%. I love you and I’ve missed you so much, I’m so happy to have you back.

Temperature 38°
Sats 95% +
Pulse 72 +
Blood pressure 92/58–107/68

Your night nurse was the lovely Cavine again.

AUTONOMIC DYSREFLEXIA (AD)

As such a dangerous medical condition, I have compiled this last chapter from experience having AD, but also from medical information from the Internet.

Other names for this condition are:

- Autonomic dysreflexia
- Hyperreflexia

Autonomic hyperreflexia is a sudden nervous system response to pain or other things that irritate the body. It can happen to people with a spinal cord injury at or above the thoracic six levels. Autonomic hyperreflexia is a medical emergency. It causes a rise in the blood pressure so high that it can cause death if not taken care of right away (2016).

High level spinal cord injuries have to deal with Autonomic Dysreflexia, this is a medical emergency risk of death.

This is where any prolonged irritation below point of injury, from a crease in clothing or ingrown toenails, squashed testicle, blocked catheter or impacted bowel cause your blood pressure to climb high without stopping, leading to a stroke or bleed in the brain and death if not acted on quickly, and with the severity of this it is wildly unknown throughout the medical authorities.

This is how I have dealt with it in my experience –

- A well-equipped emergency bag standing by with everything needed to change the catheter
- I start to hear my pulse rate
- As the pulse rises I feel it pumping around and above my right ear
- As it moves up I start feeling a headache leading to an unbearable pain with each beat of my heart, feeling like my skull cracking open
- Call 999/112/911, as with my experience – twice! They are unaware of the severity of autonomic dysreflexia and when you say "blocked catheter" they took five hours on two occasions (you can die if not acted on quickly), so… Whoever makes the emergency call needs to state first –
- My consultant and doctors told me to call stating it is a MEDICAL EMERGENCY, DANGER OF DEATH IF NOT ACTED ON IMMEDIATELY.
  - Level of injury (C5/6 tetraplegic)
  - Autonomic dysreflexia (extremely high blood pressure)
  - Ambulance required immediately (address)
  - Name and date of birth

If you or a caregiver cannot treat it promptly and correctly, it may lead to seizures, stroke and even death. Symptoms include:

- A pounding headache.
- A flushed face and/or red blotches on the skin above the level of spinal injury.

- Sweating above the level of spinal injury.
- Nasal stuffiness.
- Nausea.
- A slow heart rate (bradycardia).
- Goose bumps below the level of spinal injury.
- Cold, clammy skin below the level of spinal injury.

If you feel you have autonomic dysreflexia:

- Sit up straight, or raise your head so you are looking straight ahead. If you can lower your legs, do so. You need to be sitting upright until your blood pressure is back to normal.
- Loosen or take off any tight clothing or accessories. This includes braces, catheter tape, socks or stockings, shoes and bandages.
- Empty your bladder by draining your catheter or using your catheter.
- Use digital stimulation to empty your bowel.
- Check your skin for red spots that mean you might have a pressure injury.
- If possible, check your blood pressure every 5 minutes to see if it improves.
- Call your doctor, even if symptoms go away and your blood pressure is decreasing.
- If the symptoms return, repeat the above steps and go to the emergency room or call emergency services.

Autonomic dysreflexia occurs when something happens to your body below the level of your injury. This can be a pain or irritant (such as tight clothing or something pinching your skin) or a normal function that your body may not notice (such as having a full bladder and needing to urinate). These situations trigger an automatic reaction that causes your blood pressure to go up. As your blood pressure goes up, your heartbeat slows and may become irregular. Your body cannot restore your blood pressure to normal because of your spinal cord damage. The only way to return things to normal is to change the situation – for example, by removing tight clothing or emptying your bladder.

The following are some frequent causes of autonomic dysreflexia and how you can prevent them.

How to prevent autonomic dysreflexia –

Over full bladder
Urinary tract infections (UTIs)

- Follow your bladder management program.

Over full bowel or constipation
Gastrointestinal problems such as gallstones, stomach ulcers or gastritis

- Follow your bowel management program.
- Eat fibre and consume fluids as your doctor suggests.

Pressure injuries.
Ingrown nails.
Other skin problems.

- Check your skin daily.
- Make sure all clothing or devices fit correctly.

Sexual activity.

- Be aware that sexual activity can cause the condition. Discuss this with your doctor.

Broken bones or other injuries
Tight clothing or devices
Extreme temperatures or quick temperature changes

- Be aware that these can cause the condition. Discuss this with your doctor.
- Make sure all clothing and devices fit correctly.

Talk hard, people! Life goes on, life will always find a way.

I'm Alexander Thomas Smith signing out…

Printed in Poland
by Amazon Fulfillment
Poland Sp. z o.o., Wrocław

60566262R00067